THE LEADER'S SOUL

52 REFLECTIONS FOR UNLOCKING YOUR INNER LEADER

JAMES SHIN

Published by Freiling Agency, LLC.

P.O. Box 1264
Warrenton, VA 20188

www.FreilingAgency.com

PB ISBN: 978-1-963701-53-1
HB ISBN: 978-1-963701-54-8
E-book ISBN: 978-1-963701-55-5

Dedication

To my mom, my wife Eun Joo,
and my daughter Gabby—my greatest sources of love
and inspiration.

Contents

"

"Life is like a box of chocolates,
you never know what you're
going to get."

—*Forrest Gump*

"

Introduction

Some say life is full of surprises—and they're absolutely right.

I wrote this book because I believe life is a continuous journey of learning, growth, and discovery. Along the way, I have encountered lessons—some profound, some simple—that have shaped me into who I am today. Whether through personal experiences, professional challenges, books, movies, or even a single quote that struck a chord, these lessons have guided me through uncertainty, helped me navigate leadership, and deepened my understanding of people. I started documenting these moments, reflecting on them, and eventually writing about them. That's how this book came to be—not as a grand plan, but as a collection of insights that I hope will be helpful to others.

I was born and raised in Seoul, South Korea. On a summer day in 1994, I stood at Kimpo Airport (the only international airport before Incheon International Airport was established) with my family, preparing to leave for the U.S. I was heading to The Pennsylvania State University (Penn State) to pursue a Ph.D. in industrial engineering, but beyond that, my future was filled with uncertainty.

I didn't speak English well, had never traveled outside Korea, and knew little about American culture. Yet, I was filled with excitement and anticipation. I looked so confident that the father of another student behind me in the security line assumed I was experienced. He told me it was his son's first trip outside Korea and asked me to take care of him on the plane until we arrived in the U.S. I smiled and told him it was my first time as well. It was amusing, but more than anything, it felt like standing before a blank canvas, ready to be filled with endless possibilities.

After earning my Ph.D., I spent most of my career at Caterpillar Inc., where I moved seven times, including two international assignments. There was never a shortage of learning opportunities—both personally and professionally. I faced many challenges, but I wouldn't trade them for anything.

Throughout my journey, I've learned countless lessons, but the most important one is this: There are always good people around you—you just have to recognize them. I wouldn't have made it through some of my toughest moments without the support of the incredible people I met along the way.

Another key lesson is that people are people. I have lived in Korea, Pennsylvania, North Carolina, Illinois, Mississippi, Texas, and China, and I have traveled to numerous places globally. Regardless of background, culture, or interests, we all share fundamental human traits. These insights became the foundation of my growth and shaped me into a better leader.

My first major experience with diverse people was at Penn State. There, I had the opportunity to study and interact with students from all over the world—each representing different countries, ethnic groups, backgrounds, and languages. Coming from Korea, this exposure to a wide range of perspectives and cultures opened my eyes to the power of diversity and inclusion. Through our interactions, we learned from each other, engaged in healthy debates, and ultimately became stronger, more well-rounded individuals. The benefits of these experiences carried over into my professional life, as working with a diverse range of people and embracing different perspectives has led to better business outcomes and personal growth. This experience was especially profound for me. To this day, I maintain connections with some of the friends I made at Penn State, who remain dear to me.

Another transformative experience came during my time at Caterpillar—not from one singular moment, but through a series of invaluable experiences. During my tenure, I had the privilege of being a part of several significant corporate initiatives. I led global, cross-functional projects that not only had a substantial financial impact but also helped develop others professionally. However, one accomplishment that stands out the most was my dual role as a plant and supply chain manager in Corinth, Mississippi.

Corinth, a small town of about 15,000 people, presented unique challenges, but it was also where I made some of my most meaningful contributions. I take great pride in the personal impact I had on employees and the positive changes we achieved together. This experience not only helped me grow as a leader but also allowed me to make a real difference in people's lives. I formed lasting friendships, and to this day, we remain in touch, reminiscing about our shared experiences. Looking back, there's no doubt that the experience helped me become a better person.

As I grew into a better person, I began opening my eyes and ears to inspirational things. These could be lessons on what to do, what not to do, or ways to strengthen myself. Inspiration came from the simplest things—a movie, a book, or a quote. Sometimes, it was a significant life event or the small, everyday moments that constantly shaped me. I started noticing these things more, observing them, and taking note. Eventually, I began writing about them, and I never stopped. That's how I arrived at this point.

I hope these little stories are helpful to you and that some resonate with your own experiences. Much of this is especially for young professionals who have just embarked on their careers. As someone who has walked this path before, I hope my experiences provide guidance for your journey or serve as a point of reflection down the road. In my view, one of the most crucial pieces of advice is to broaden your horizons and gain as much experience as possible during this unique stage of your life.

Among many important areas to focus on, I highly recommend two in particular.

First, building a strong professional network and seeking out mentorship and sponsorship can be invaluable. You can establish a network by fostering relationships within your organization, joining professional groups, or volunteering at events outside of your immediate field. Remember, networking is a two-way street—it benefits everyone involved. Don't hesitate to reach out for advice or assistance; some of the people you connect with may even become your mentors or sponsors. Be proactive, take initiative, and embrace new opportunities. Additionally, stepping outside your comfort zone and seeking new experiences will help you grow both professionally and personally.

Second, maintaining a healthy work-life balance—however you define it—is essential for long-term success and well-being. This topic can be controversial, but it is essential to prioritize your life over your profession when faced with conflicting situations. Maintaining good mental and physical health is important for achieving a balanced lifestyle. It is necessary to be disciplined in setting and sticking to your priorities, and you can improve by practicing it regularly and making it a habit, just like exercising a muscle. Achieving a healthy work-life balance is not easy, but it is achievable and is crucial for your success professionally and personally.

For those ahead of me or from an earlier generation, I hope your experiences were even better than mine. But at the very least, these are moments we can share and relate to.

More than anything, I hope this book encourages you to reflect, grow, and embrace the journey ahead with an open mind and a full heart.

"Leadership is not about being in charge. It is about taking care of those in your charge."

—*Simon Sinek*

1

The Weight of Leadership

Authentic leadership isn't about titles, authority, or power—it's about responsibility. It's about standing in the gap for those you lead, shielding them when necessary, and taking the heat so they can do their best work. True leadership isn't about personal recognition; it's about creating an environment where others can succeed.

Leadership Comes with Battle Scars

While reading *Loonshots*, I came across a powerful quote from Dr. Judah Folkman:

> "You can tell a leader by counting the number of arrows in his ass."

At first glance, it's humorous. But beneath the humor lies a profound truth. Leadership comes with battle scars. The more responsibility you take on, the more criticism, resistance, and setbacks you will face. Those arrows? They represent the challenges, doubts, and pushback that every leader must endure.

But here's what separates real leaders: they don't back down. They don't let the arrows define them or defeat them. Instead, they learn from every setback, becoming wiser, more resilient, and better equipped to lead.

Great leaders also serve as a shield for their teams. They absorb external pressures so their people can stay focused on the mission. They take the brunt of criticism, deflect unnecessary distractions, and create an environment where their teams can thrive. And when the team succeeds, so does the leader.

Martin Luther King Jr. put it best: "The ultimate measure of a man is not where he stands in moments of comfort and convenience, but where he stands at times of challenge and controversy."

So the next time you feel the weight of leadership—the resistance, the criticism, the setbacks—remember: every challenge is an opportunity to grow stronger. Every arrow is a sign that you're in the fight, doing the hard work that leadership demands.

How do you respond to the arrows that come with leadership?

"Ancora imparo.
(I am still learning.)"

—*Michelangelo, age 87*

2

Lead With Curiosity

Although I don't have musical talent myself, I live in a home full of musicians. My wife is a professional pianist, and music is a frequent topic of conversation around our table. Not long ago, she shared a story with me about Pablo Casals—one of the most influential musicians of the 20th century. Casals was not only a renowned cellist but also a gifted conductor and composer. When asked why he still practiced daily in his 80s, his answer was as humble as it was powerful: he said he was still improving.

There are a few versions of this exchange, but the most widely quoted one goes something like this:

A journalist, amazed by Casals's discipline and dedication, asked him:

"Mr. Casals, you are the greatest cellist who has ever lived. Why do you still practice four to five hours a day?"

Casals replied,

"Because I think I'm making progress."

Though the exact source of the quote isn't entirely clear—perhaps from the 1966 short film *A Day in the Life of Pablo Casals*—what's undeniable is the spirit behind his words. Casals repeated this idea throughout his life, and the message remains timeless: even in the twilight of his career, he was committed to growth. He believed there was always room to improve.

The Never-Ending Climb Toward Mastery

Casals isn't alone in this belief. Jiro Ono, the legendary Japanese sushi chef, once remarked in his 80s, "Even at my age, in my work… I haven't reached perfection."

It's a sentiment echoed by many of the world's greatest artists, athletes, and thinkers: mastery is not a destination—it's a lifelong journey. Talent can only take you so far. Without ongoing learning and deliberate practice, skills can fade. True greatness comes from sustained effort, humility, and a relentless pursuit of excellence.

That's why lifelong learning matters. It reminds us that no matter how skilled or successful we become, there is always more to explore, refine, and understand. Progress is always possible—if we keep showing up.

Learning Is Living

But the benefits of lifelong learning extend far beyond professional achievement. Staying curious and mentally engaged supports both emotional well-being and physical health. Studies show that learning new skills can sharpen cognitive function, reduce the risk of diseases like Alzheimer's, and even reduce stress. Social engagement through learning has also been tied to a longer, more fulfilling life.

In short, lifelong learning isn't just good for your career—it's good for your soul.

There's no expiration date on growth. No age limit for curiosity. Whether you're learning to play the cello, run a business, lead a team, or simply live a richer life, the key is to never stop learning.

What are *you* most curious about?

What do *you* want to keep improving?

> "As I see it, the most critical role I have is to make sure that I leave the business better than I found it and to turn it over to more capable hands when I leave."
>
> —*Ed Rapp, Former Group President, Caterpillar*

3

Leading Beyond Yourself

This quote from Ed Rapp perfectly captures the essence of authentic leadership—creating a lasting impact, not just short-term results. The mark of a great leader isn't how indispensable they become but how well they prepare others to succeed in their absence.

Too often, young professionals focus solely on climbing the ladder, chasing promotions, and proving their individual worth. While ambition is valuable, leadership is not about being irreplaceable—it's about developing others so that the organization thrives long after you're gone. It may seem counterintuitive, but the more you invest in training and empowering others, the more valuable you become.

Skill and competence are essential, but they must be recognized to be effective. Being great at your work isn't enough if no one knows about it. Actively engaging in high-impact projects, volunteering for challenges, and demonstrating value in visible ways will establish your reputation as a leader.

At the same time, growth requires boldness. Progress isn't made by staying within the bounds of comfort. Taking initiative, embracing calculated risks, and showing the courage to step up—even when failure is a possibility—are the hallmarks of professionals who rise to leadership roles.

The Leadership Imperative: Integrity and Compassion

As I reflect on the qualities that define strong leadership, many attributes come to mind. But two stand out above the rest: Integrity and Compassion.

- Integrity is the foundation of trust. Without it, leadership crumbles. A leader's word must mean something, and their actions must align with their values.
- Compassion is what connects leaders to their teams. It's the ability to understand and care for those you lead, creating an environment where people feel valued, supported, and empowered.

These qualities and business competence form the backbone of effective leadership. Leaders who embody integrity and compassion achieve great results and build strong, inspired teams that continue to excel long after they've moved on.

Sheryl Sandberg wrote, "Leadership is about making others better as a result of your presence and making sure that impact lasts in your absence." Indeed, success isn't just about what you accomplish—it's about the legacy you leave behind. Make it one worth following.

What steps are you taking today to ensure that your leadership leaves a lasting impact beyond your tenure?

"If you don't know what you want,
you'll never find it."

—*Unknown*

4

Knowing What "Good" Looks Like

I love cooking, and whenever I get the chance, I enjoy watching documentaries about food. In an episode of *Ugly Delicious*, chef David Chang had a conversation with pizza restaurateur Mark Iacono.

David: Is it cheesy to say that it'll be delicious if you put love into food?

Mark: No. No, no, no. You still need to know what good pizza tastes like.

This exchange stuck with me because it highlights a crucial truth: effort and passion alone aren't enough to achieve excellence. You can work tirelessly, but if you don't clearly understand what "good" looks like, you may never reach your full potential.

Imagine a pizza chef who spends years perfecting their technique but has no sense of what makes a great pizza. They might work hard, but their results may never meet the highest standards without a clear benchmark. The same applies in any profession—success isn't just about persistence; it's about knowing what you're aiming for.

How Do You Develop an Understanding of Excellence?

- Benchmark Against the Best – Compare your work to industry leaders and high performers. Studying excellence helps refine your standards and gives you something to aspire to.
- Learn from Experienced Professionals – Mentorship and collaboration with accomplished individuals provide firsthand exposure to what works and what doesn't.
- Commit to Lifelong Learning – Excellence isn't static. As industries evolve, so do the benchmarks for success. Staying ahead requires continuous education, adaptation, and growth.

Excellence Is a Foundation for Innovation

Understanding what "good" looks like doesn't mean stifling creativity. Instead, it provides a foundation for innovation. A skilled chef who understands the fundamentals of flavor can experiment boldly while still producing exceptional dishes. Likewise, in business and leadership, those who master the basics can push boundaries and drive meaningful progress.

Excellence isn't achieved by accident. It requires dedication, knowledge, and a clear vision of success. Without that clarity, you risk aimless effort. But when you know what "good" looks like, you have a roadmap to guide you toward excellence. Like Yogi Berra once said, "If you don't know where you are going, you'll end up someplace else!"

What steps are you taking to define and refine your standard of excellence?

"It is not that we have
a short time to live, but that
we waste a lot of it."

— *Seneca*

5

The Productivity of Life

We often talk about time management, but do we genuinely measure how effectively we use our time? Overall Equipment Effectiveness (OEE) in manufacturing is a critical metric that measures machine productivity—essentially, how much of its operating time is genuinely productive. This concept isn't just for factory floors; it also applies to our lives.

A leader I greatly admire once challenged me: "As a leader, measure your personal OEE." In other words, look at your calendar. How much of your time is spent on what truly matters? How often are you engaged in high-impact activities versus distractions? A practical way to improve is to block time for your priorities, whether strategic thinking, personal development, or well-being.

Life Must Take Precedence Over Work

I once discussed this idea in an interview with the Graduate School at Penn State, where we explored the delicate balance between professional ambition and personal well-being. While it may seem controversial to some, the reality is that life must take precedence over work when conflicts arise.

No job title, promotion, or career milestone is worth sacrificing your mental and physical health. Without a strong foundation of well-being, even the most remarkable professional achievements can become unsustainable, leading to burnout, dissatisfaction, or even regret.

Prioritization Is a Discipline

Prioritization is not just a one-time decision—it's a discipline, much like training a muscle. It requires conscious effort, regular reflection, and the courage to set boundaries. Jim Rohn once wrote, "Take care of your body; it's the only place you have to live." If time is your most valuable resource, use it wisely. Maintaining work-life balance isn't just about reducing stress—it's about ensuring long-term success and fulfillment. It's not easy, but it is possible through small, continuous improvements. Success—whether in work or life—isn't about doing more; it's about doing what matters most.

How effectively are you using your time, and what changes could help you focus on what truly matters?

"There are two secrets in cooking.
One is to buy the best materials,
and the second is not
to spoil them."

— *Uri Buri*

6

The Recipe for Talent Management

I n *Somebody Feed Phil*, an episode on Tel Aviv featured renowned chef Uri Buri, who shared this simple yet profound insight. It makes perfect sense in the kitchen, but it also applies to a completely different arena—talent management. Just as great cooking starts with high-quality ingredients and the skill to enhance them, building a high-performing team requires identifying the right talent and nurturing it effectively.

Talent management is what separates average companies from truly exceptional ones. It's not just about hiring the best people—it's about developing, refining, and maximizing their potential. The process begins with spotting raw talent, often an early indicator of future leadership. But talent alone isn't enough. Like kitchen ingredients, potential must be cultivated, seasoned, and prepared to bring out the best results.

Once talent is identified, the next step is structured training, mentorship, and exposure to diverse experiences. Learning from seasoned professionals, engaging in challenging projects, and gaining hands-on experience all refine skills and foster innovation. Providing opportunities for employees to showcase their abilities not only accelerates growth but also helps them establish credibility within the company and industry.

The Role of a Leader: The Master Chef

There is no one-size-fits-all approach to talent management. As a leader, your job is like that of a chef—you must create your own recipe for success. Each employee brings unique strengths, and it's your role to blend them together to create the most effective and high-performing team. Some individuals may thrive with direct mentorship, while others flourish with autonomy and creative freedom. Recognizing these nuances is what turns a leader into a true master of talent development.

And remember, failing to invest in talent is a recipe for disaster. As Henry Ford wisely put it, "The only thing worse than training your employees and having them leave is not training them and having them stay." Like a great dish, a successful organization is built on the quality of its ingredients and the skill with which they are brought together. Handle your talent well, and your company will thrive.

How are you cultivating and developing the talent within your team to bring out their full potential?

"Efforts and courage are not enough without purpose and direction."

—*John F. Kennedy*

7

Start With Purpose, Not Just Process

Simon Sinek's powerful concept of "Start with Why" has reshaped the way we think about leadership, business, and motivation. At the core of his idea is a simple but profound distinction: *why* you do something matters more than *what* you do or *how* you do it.

Sinek introduces this through his "Golden Circle" framework, made up of three layers:

- **What** – This is what you do. Your product, service, or job.
- **How** – This is how you do it. Your unique processes or methods.
- **Why** – This is your purpose. The belief or cause that drives you.

Most people and companies can clearly describe what they do. Some can explain how they do it. But only a few can articulate their *why*—and those who do are often the ones who stand out, inspire, and lead lasting change.

Why is "why" so powerful? Because people don't buy *what* you do—they buy *why* you do it. Purpose connects on an emotional level. It creates loyalty, meaning, and impact.

Consider Apple. They don't just sell laptops and phones. Their "why" is to challenge the status quo and think differently. Martin Luther King Jr. didn't say, "I have a plan." He said, "I have a dream." That's the power of purpose—it moves people.

Purpose Drives Culture, Connection, and Growth

When I encounter poor customer service or disengaged employees, it's usually a sign that the organization has lost touch with its *why*. Without a clear and compelling purpose, work becomes transactional. Culture suffers. Teams drift. And customers feel the difference.

Strong leadership starts with defining and living the "why." It's what fuels innovation, strengthens internal culture, and builds trust externally. It gives employees a reason to show up beyond a paycheck. It turns customers into fans. And it helps organizations stay focused and aligned—even in times of uncertainty.

Zappos is a great example. Their "why" is to deliver happiness to customers and employees. That purpose is embedded in everything they do, from hiring to customer service to leadership development. As a result, they've built a brand known for joy, loyalty, and long-term success.

When your "why" is clear, performance improves, communication gets sharper, and people care more. It boosts morale, reduces turnover, and drives better business outcomes. And the best part? It's sustainable.

So, what's your *why*? Why do you lead, serve, or build? What is the deeper motivation behind your work?

"An ounce of prevention is worth a pound of cure."

—*Benjamin Franklin*

8

Planning Ahead: The Key to Long-Term Success

You've probably heard the saying, "Measure twice, cut once." It's a simple yet powerful rule in woodworking—double-check your measurements before cutting to avoid costly mistakes. If a cut is too short, you waste materials. If it's too long, you have to start over. But this principle extends far beyond carpentry—it applies to decision-making, business strategies, and even personal growth.

Why am I saying this? I see this principle play out in continuous improvement methodologies, particularly through the Six Sigma's DMAIC process: Define, Measure, Analyze, Improve, and Control. Confused? Let me simplify. While Six Sigma is about statistics and quality control, that's also an oversimplification. It's a powerful, practical method that helps businesses run better by finding and fixing problems, reducing mistakes, and improving how things work. Learning Six Sigma gives you valuable tools to solve problems and grow in your career, no matter what industry you're in.

At its core, Six Sigma is about three key principles:

1. Delivering value to the customer
2. Engaging employees
3. Developing future leaders

By implementing structured processes like DMAIC, organizations can avoid wasted effort and unnecessary rework—essentially ensuring that when the time comes to act, they do it right the first time.

The Power of Proactive Problem-Solving

Let's break down how this works:

- **Define:** What is the problem?
- **Measure:** Where are we now?
- **Analyze:** What are the root causes?
- **Improve:** What is the solution?
- **Control:** How do we sustain the gains?

Following this approach ensures that organizations don't just react to problems as they arise but actively prevent them from occurring in the first place. It's the business equivalent of "Measure twice, cut once"— or perhaps even more accurately, "Measure once, cut once."

When we invest time upfront in planning and prevention, we save ourselves from costly mistakes down the road. Whether in business, leadership, or personal endeavors, taking a disciplined, proactive approach can mean the difference between success and struggle.

What area of your life or work could benefit from a more structured, preventative approach?

"Water does not resist.
Water flows. When you pour
water into a cup, it becomes the
cup. When you pour water into a
bottle, it becomes the bottle. When
you pour water in a teapot,
it becomes the teapot."

—*Bruce Lee*

9

The Wisdom of Water

I'd like to share a philosophical message from Laozi: 上善若水, which translates to "The Highest Good is Like Water"

Laozi was an ancient Chinese philosopher, and this expression comes from his book, the "Dao De Jing (道德经)", which emphasizes living in harmony with the Dao (道), or "the Way," a fundamental principle underlying the universe.

The full passage states:

上善若水。水善利万物而不争，处众人之所恶，故几于道。

(The highest good is like water. It benefits all things without competing. It willingly dwells in places that people disdain, and in doing so, it aligns with the Dao)

What We Can Learn From Water

Laozi taught that the best way to live is to be like water. Water possesses great power, yet it remains humble and flows with a gentle expression. He urged people to learn from the wisdom of water.

1. Water is adaptable: When poured into a square container, it takes a square shape; when poured into a round container, it takes a round shape. No matter the situation, water maintains its essence while adjusting to its surroundings.
2. Water has immense power. In its calm state, water flows through valleys, nourishes trees and vegetation, and quenches the thirst of animals. Yet, when it surges, it can shatter rocks and bring down mountains.
3. Water flows downward. It always seeks the lowest place, never resisting gravity. Flowing lower and lower, it ultimately reaches the vast ocean.

These are the reasons Laozi described water as the most virtuous force in the world. In life, we are not like water—it is not always easy to embody its qualities as we face daily challenges and struggles. However, we can learn valuable lessons from water:

- We can be adaptable, allowing us to be more flexible and resilient.

- Though we can be calm, we must also cultivate inner strength to stand firm in our values and foundations.
- Most importantly, we should remain humble and treat others with respect.

Can you be like water today?

"

"If you get on the wrong train, get off at the nearest station. The longer it takes you to get off, the more expensive the return trip will be."

—*Unknown*

"

10

Recognizing When You're on the Wrong Train

L ife is a journey filled with choices—some planned, others unexpected. At times, we may find ourselves on a path that no longer aligns with our values, goals, or happiness. Whether it's a job that drains us, a relationship that no longer brings joy, or a pursuit that has lost its meaning, staying on the wrong train only prolongs frustration and regret. The sooner we recognize that we need a course correction, the easier it is to pivot toward a better direction.

Making the decision to step off the wrong train is often difficult. We might convince ourselves that if we stay a little longer, things will improve. We may justify our inaction with thoughts like, *I've already invested too much time* or *What if leaving makes things worse?* The truth is, the longer we delay, the more we entrench ourselves in a situation that isn't serving us, and the cost of change becomes even greater.

The Cost of Delayed Change

Every extra stop on the wrong train is time, energy, and resources lost. The longer we stay in a situation that isn't right for us, the harder it becomes to leave. This is often due to a psychological principle called the *sunk cost fallacy*—the tendency to continue investing in something simply because we've already put in so much. However, what's done is done, and staying out of fear of wasted time will only lead to more regret in the future.

I've had my share of wrong trains. There were times when I stayed in situations far longer than I should have, hoping things would improve. But when I finally had the courage to step off and redirect my path, I realized that those difficult decisions were necessary for my personal and professional growth. While making those changes came at a cost, staying would have been even costlier. Looking back, I see that those decisions, though painful at the time, were among the best I've made.

Embracing Course Corrections

Life is about learning, adapting, and growing. Making mistakes is inevitable, but what truly matters is how we respond to them. When we recognize that we're heading in the wrong direction, we have the power to change course. Sometimes, that means taking a leap into the unknown, trusting that the discomfort of transition is better than the pain of staying stuck.

Are you on the right train heading toward your true destination, or is it time to get off and find a better path?

"Sometimes you need to push yourself, but you also need to know when to step back and give yourself a break. Rest is just as important as progress."

—*Arianna Huffington*

11

Knowing When to Push and When to Pause

What is your personal "2 o'clock rule"? In climbing Mt. Everest, there is a well-known rule that climbers must reach the summit by 2 pm due to the harsh weather conditions that follow. If they fail to do so, the descent becomes dangerously treacherous, increasing the risk of fatal consequences. Ignoring this rule has led to tragedies, including the infamous 1996 disaster detailed in *Into Thin Air* by Jon Krakauer. Climbers Rob Hall and Scott Fischer pushed past their safe window, only to be caught in a sudden blizzard, which ultimately led to their deaths and the loss of eight others.

On the other hand, the 2015 documentary *Meru* tells a different story. In 2008, climbers Conrad Anker, Jimmy Chin, and Renan Ozturk attempted to conquer the Shark's Fin route on India's Meru Peak. Just 100 meters from the summit, brutal weather forced them to turn back. While many would have seen this as a failure, their decision to retreat preserved their safety, allowing them to return and successfully complete the climb three years later.

The Balance Between Persistence and Wisdom

These stories illustrate an essential lesson: while perseverance is often praised, knowing when to pause or change direction is just as crucial. The "2 o'clock rule" isn't just for extreme mountaineering—it applies to life, business, and personal growth.

There are times when pushing forward is necessary, but there are also moments when stepping back is the wisest course of action. Whether it's reevaluating a business strategy, adjusting career plans, or prioritizing health and family, pausing at the right moment can be the difference between sustainable success and unnecessary setbacks.

A long time ago, I read a short story in *Reader's Digest* about salmon swimming upstream in Alaska. Near the main river, the writer discovered a pond where exhausted salmon paused to rest before completing their final journey. The story compared this natural pause to human life, reminding us that constantly pushing forward without rest can lead to burnout, making the pursuit of success meaningless.

Defining Your Own "2 O'clock Rule"

Unlike the rigid rule in Everest climbing, our personal "2 o'clock" moments are unique to each situation. It might be a specific deadline, a major life event, or simply a feeling that tells you it's time to reassess. Recognizing these moments and acting on them can make all the difference in long-term success.

What is your personal "2 o'clock rule"—the moment when you should pause, reassess, or change direction before pushing forward?

"The greatest mistake you can make in life is to be continually fearing you will make one."

—*Elbert Hubbard*

12

The Music Beyond the Notes

As a musical family, we got to know a distinguished violinst in his 80s who had many interesting musical experiences, including encounters with renowned musicians. One day, he recounted attending a concert by the famous pianist Clifford Curzon in London many years ago. Curzon played *Piano Concerto No. 1 in B-flat minor* by Tchaikovsky, delivering an extraordinary performance despite missing an entire passage of notes. From this, the teacher imparted a profound lesson: "You can miss notes, but not the music."

In music, hitting a wrong note here or there is relatively inconsequential as long as the overall composition and artistic expression remain intact. A single flawed note does not necessarily ruin the entire performance. The key is not allowing minor mistakes to derail the flow or cause the performer to lose track of delivering the intended experience.

Shifting Focus from Perfection to Progress

This idea extends beyond music into many areas of life. We may falter or make mistakes, but if we stay committed to the broader vision, the essence of what we're striving for can still shine through. Fixating on small flaws can distract from the bigger picture and hinder progress.

In any complex endeavor, perfection is rarely attainable. Yet, excessive self-criticism over small errors can lead to frustration and hesitation. The wisdom in "You can miss notes, but not the music" lies in recognizing that small mistakes don't define the entire journey. Instead of fearing failure, embracing the process and learning from missteps can lead to greater resilience and creativity.

Embracing the Bigger Picture

This philosophy serves as an antidote to defeatist thinking, encouraging perseverance even when setbacks occur. Whether in business, leadership, or personal growth, mistakes are inevitable. The key is ensuring they don't overshadow the broader mission.

The best musicians, athletes, and leaders all understand this: true excellence is not about never making mistakes, but about how quickly and effectively you recover from them. The melody of success is composed not by avoiding errors but by staying committed to the vision despite them.

What areas of your life require you to focus less on individual mistakes and more on the bigger picture?

"A recipe has no soul.
You, as the cook, must bring soul
to the recipe."

—*Thomas Keller*

13

The Art of Cooking and Leadership

You can learn a lot about leadership from cooking. Curious? Let me explain. First, I have control over the quality of ingredients used, ensuring I only incorporate fresh, wholesome items. Second, there's an excitement in witnessing the transformation of separate components into a delectable final dish. One meal I make quite frequently is pizza, which happens to be my daughter's favorite food. The beauty of homemade pizza lies in its simplicity. It's not only economical but can also be quite healthy, requiring just a handful of simple ingredients.

In a previous article, I quoted a chef who shared two cooking secrets: using the best quality ingredients and not spoiling them during preparation. I would add a third crucial aspect—understanding the role each ingredient plays in contributing flavor, texture, and aroma. Interestingly, these culinary elements bear striking parallels to effective talent management.

Selecting and Blending the Right Ingredients

Just as a chef selects ingredients tailored to a specific dish, as a leader, it's imperative to discern the right talent for each role. Recognizing that an "A" player isn't always necessary underscores the importance of matching skills and personalities to the demands of the position.

Much like assembling ingredients for a recipe, crafting a successful team necessitates aligning talents with roles. An organizational structure should remain fluid, adapting to the unique strengths of its people. Addressing talent gaps involves a strategic blend of recruitment and internal development, emphasizing the importance of strong talent management and succession planning.

Nurturing and Developing Talent

Just as mishandling ingredients can ruin a dish, neglecting talent by placing individuals in ill-fitting roles or failing to provide ongoing development opportunities can undermine organizational success. Ensuring people are in roles that leverage their strengths while fostering their continuous growth is essential. As Richard Branson aptly noted, "Train people well enough so they can leave. Treat them well enough so they don't want to."

In essence, effective leadership mirrors the craft of cooking. Like a skilled chef, a leader must curate their own "recipe," defining what success looks like, blending diverse talents as unique "ingredients" to create exceptional results. Talent management, much like cooking, hinges on understanding, nurturing, and maximizing the potential of each element to create a truly successful outcome.

How are you refining your leadership "recipe" to bring out the best in your team?

"

"Life moves pretty fast. If you don't stop and look around once in a while, you could miss it."

—Ferris Bueller's Day Off

"

14

Finding Stillness in the Fast-Paced World

Behind my house in Illinois, three decent-sized ponds served as an unexpected sanctuary. Though it was a residential area, the ponds attracted a remarkable variety of wildlife. I often ran or walked along the paths surrounding them, allowing me to observe nature in ways I might have otherwise overlooked.

Canada geese were common visitors, frequently stopping during their migration. Great Blue Herons, with their striking presence, became regulars as well—I even managed to capture moments of one catching fish with my camera. The rarest sight was a Great Egret, which I only spotted a few times. Strangely, a pelican couple once made an appearance, an unusual sighting for the area. Muskrats also made their home in the ponds, occasionally seen swimming or munching on grass.

Unexpected Encounters with Wildlife

One particularly memorable experience involved a Snow Goose. Unlike its usual nature of traveling in large flocks, this one was completely alone. I had never seen one before and had to research what it was. Over the months, I took many pictures of this beautiful bird. It spent most of its time in solitude but occasionally kept company with a Canada Goose before eventually disappearing.

Another time, while on a run, I noticed a small, dried, clay-like ball. Upon closer inspection, I realized it was a tiny turtle. Unsure if it was still alive, I carefully placed it into the pond. A few seconds later, it came to life, staring at me from the water. I could only wonder what it was thinking—perhaps a moment of appreciation, or maybe just confusion. Regardless, I was happy to have saved it.

One of the most striking moments happened just as I was leaving Caterpillar after 20 years of service. On that very day, I saw a small rabbit trapped between my neighbor's fence. The fence bars were narrower than usual since they had small dogs. The rabbit was frantic, its side bloody, and its tail missing—likely the result of a hawk attack. I didn't see the predator, but I assumed it had flown away as I approached. With some effort, I freed the rabbit, and it sprinted away. That moment, happening on such a significant day, felt symbolic—almost as if life itself was showing me that even in moments of transition, there is always an opportunity to make a difference.

Lessons from Nature

Observing nature became more than just a pastime—it provided me with moments of reflection, clarity, and renewal. Despite professional challenges and a hectic schedule, these experiences reminded me to slow down, appreciate the world around me, and find beauty in unexpected places.

From hawks soaring through the sky to tiny tree frogs clinging to my second-story window, each moment carried a lesson. Nature doesn't rush, yet everything is accomplished in its own time.

It makes me wonder: Have you stopped and looked around today?

"Leadership is not about
being fearless. It's about making
tough decisions despite your fears."

—*Unknown*

15

Fear Is a Sign of Responsibility

As I mentioned earlier, my wife is a professional pianist, and my daughter plays the violin, so classical music is always in my home. Recently, they watched an episode of *Living the Classical Life* on YouTube titled *For Me, Life is Beginning at Ninety featuring* Seymour Bernstein, and they shared it with me.

Seymour Bernstein, born in 1927, is a renowned pianist, composer, and teacher who has left a significant mark on the music world. The phrase *For me, life is beginning at ninety* reflects his perspective on aging as an ongoing journey of personal growth and fulfillment. In the episode, Bernstein recounted a conversation with actor and director Ethan Hawke, who admitted to experiencing stage fright. Bernstein's response was simple but profound:

> "As I explained to Ethan Hawke, you should be proud because it's a sign that you're responsible. If you were irresponsible, you wouldn't experience it."

Leadership, in all its forms, is similar. Fear is a natural emotion; rather than being ashamed, leaders should see it as a sign of responsibility. Making decisions, especially when leading other leaders, can be daunting. However, by embracing and acknowledging these emotions, leaders can transform them into self-confidence and growth.

Developing Others Is the Heart of Leadership

Bernstein also spoke about his love of teaching, saying:

> "I adored teaching. Do you know what I love best about teaching? I love the feeling of making a pupil feel good about themselves. You know they can play a certain passage, and I practice with them and get them to play that passage, and they are elated. They can't believe that they're actually able to do it, and I get 10 times more reward from their pleasure. And that's one of the great things about teaching. You make people better."

This perfectly parallels leadership. Developing others is at the heart of what great leaders do. A leader must carefully cultivate their team, just as a teacher nurtures students or a musician refines a performance. Understanding the unique strengths and challenges of each team member—much like understanding musical notes and rhythms—allows a leader to bring out the best in others and shape an organization's future.

Leadership Is an Art

In the final moments of the episode, pianist Zsolt Bognár asked Bernstein a powerful question:

"A hundred years from now, when we're all gone, how would you like to be remembered— as a pianist and teacher?"

Bernstein responded without hesitation:

"As a person. I want to be remembered for everything I'm trying to project now regarding human relationships because that's what life is all about. We're relating to other people. We want to give the best of ourselves to others and make them feel good about themselves. That's what I want to be remembered for doing."

This response highlights two of the most over- looked yet essential leadership qualities: humility and empathy. While performance and execution are important, they must be guided by a deeper purpose— helping others grow, fostering meaningful connec- tions, and leading with integrity.

I often share this quote by John C. Maxwell:

"The true measure of leadership is how well you prepare others to carry on in your absence."

That is the essence of true leadership. Much like music, leadership is not just about execution—it is about inspiration, creativity, and human connection. It is, in every sense, an art.

How are you using your leadership to develop and uplift others?

"You don't have to be a hero to accomplish great things—to compete. You can just be an ordinary chap, sufficiently motivated to reach challenging goals."

—*Sir Edmund Hillary*

16

Lessons from the Climb

During my short trip to Japan in 2024, I had the opportunity to climb Mt. Fuji (3,776m / 12,389ft)—a long-time bucket list item for me. While it may be an easier climb for some, it was a humbling experience that provided plenty of time for reflection. As I made my way up, I found that the climb offered life lessons extending far beyond the mountain.

Preparation Is Key

Feeling out of shape, I committed to a regular workout routine leading up to the climb. I also prepared for unpredictable weather and gathered essential equipment, including rain gear, walking sticks, and proper clothing. In hindsight, every bit of preparation mattered. Life often throws unexpected challenges, but solid groundwork can make the journey smoother.

The Importance of Pacing and Helping Others

Early in the climb, I realized that pacing myself was critical. My endurance was better than I expected, so I initially pushed forward too fast, reaching Station 8 quickly (with Station 10 being the summit). But I soon realized that this pace wasn't sustainable. Adjusting my speed allowed me to preserve energy and finish strong—a valuable reminder that sometimes, slowing down is essential for achieving long-term goals.

After Station 8, I encountered a fellow climber who was struggling. I chose to slow down further and help them reach the top. It extended my climb, but I wouldn't change that decision. Climbing Mt. Fuji wasn't about racing ahead—it was about the journey and the people we meet along the way. Success is rarely just about personal achievement; it's about growth and supporting others.

This experience also reinforced another lesson: everyone's journey is different. Some climb faster, some struggle, and some need encouragement. Life is much the same—our pace doesn't define our success, but how we navigate challenges and lift others along the way does.

Gratitude and Looking Ahead

I'm deeply grateful to my friend, Hikaru Suzuki, who hosted my trip, assisted with preparation, and climbed alongside me. Our engaging business, culture, and life conversations made the experience even more memorable.

Looking back, this climb was more than a personal accomplishment—it was a lesson in patience, preparation, and perseverance. And while I'm proud of reaching the summit, I'm already thinking about my next adventure. In the meantime, I'm preparing to climb Mt. Fuji again!

What personal challenge or goal has taught you valuable life lessons?

"

"It is not the strongest of the species
that survive, nor the most intelligent,
but the one most responsive
to change."

—*Charles Darwin*

"

17

The Balance Between Strategy and Adaptability

Congratulations to the Dodgers on winning the 2024 World Championship! Their victory was an incredible achievement and a reminder of how adaptability plays a crucial role in success.

Their win brought to mind *Moneyball* by Michael Lewis, a book about how the underfunded Oakland A's used innovative strategies to compete at a high level. Led by GM Billy Beane, the A's relied on overlooked metrics like on-base percentage to find undervalued players, challenging traditional scouting methods, and building a competitive team on a limited budget.

The Dodgers, with a much higher payroll, aren't a typical *Moneyball* example, but the book highlights an important limitation of a purely statistical approach, especially in the playoffs. Lewis notes that while sabermetrics gives teams an edge over a long regular season, the playoffs are different. Short series and high-stakes games introduce unpredictable factors where a single play, a streak of bad luck, or an unexpected slump can determine outcomes.

When Adaptability Beats Data

The Dodgers' championship run proved this point. Shohei Ohtani, one of the team's biggest stars, struggled in the playoffs, but unexpected heroes like Tommy Edmon and an injured Freddie Freeman stepped up. Manager Dave Roberts adjusted his approach, leaning heavily on bullpen management—a strategy he may not have used as aggressively during the regular season. Conversely, the Yankees' stars underperformed, and unforced errors in Game 5 sealed the series' fate.

This lesson extends beyond baseball. Data-driven strategies work exceptionally well in routine, stable environments but often struggle in high-stakes, unpredictable situations.

For example, companies optimize supply chains for efficiency, but recent disruptions—the pandemic, geopolitical tensions, natural disasters, and strikes— have exposed the dangers of inflexibility. Businesses that relied solely on lean (waste elimination), cost-efficient operations without backup plans suffered the most. Those that incorporated flexibility, redundancy, and alternative sourcing were better positioned to adapt.

The Art of Blending Data and Flexibility

There's no question that data provides a strategic advantage in long-term planning and optimization. But in crisis situations or unpredictable, high-stakes environments, traditional strengths like human intuition, flexibility, and contingency planning often become essential. The key to long-term success lies in balancing data-driven decision-making and adaptability.

This is true in sports, business, and leadership. Strategy can set you up for success, but when things don't go as planned—as they often don't—your ability to adjust and respond will define your outcome.

How do you balance data-driven strategies with adaptability in your work or life?

"A nation's culture resides in the hearts and in the soul of its people."

—*Mahatma Gandhi*

18

Understanding Culture Beyond Words

I have been fortunate to travel to many countries and experience diverse cultures and customs. One of my favorite ways to connect with a new place is through its local cuisine—sharing a meal often provides a deeper understanding of culture than words ever could. These experiences have been personally enriching and valuable in business, where cultural awareness fosters stronger relationships and more effective collaboration.

The Importance of Cultural Awareness

However, unfamiliarity with a culture can lead to unintentional mistakes, even if made with good intentions. A small but interesting example is the 'V' finger gesture. In many cultures, holding up a 'V' sign with the palm facing outward is widely recognized as a symbol of peace or victory, popularized around World War II. But if the same gesture is made with the palm facing inward, it can be offensive in countries like the UK, Ireland, Australia, and New Zealand. Even Winston Churchill reportedly made this mistake in the early days before adjusting how he used the gesture.

Curious about this, I once researched a popular theory—though unconfirmed—about its origins. It dates back to medieval times, specifically during the Hundred Years' War between England and France. According to legend, English archers would make this gesture to signal they still had their two crucial fingers—the index and middle—essential for drawing a bow. French captors were rumored to cut off these fingers if archers were caught, preventing them from ever shooting again. While historians debate the accuracy of this story, it remains a widely accepted explanation. Fascinating, isn't it?

The Power of Learning and Connection

Cultural awareness is invaluable, especially in today's globally connected world. By understanding the nuances of gestures, traditions, and customs, we show respect, avoid unintended offense, and create smoother, more meaningful in—person and professional interactions. Every culture has its unique way of communicating, often beyond just words, and those who take the time to learn about these differences build deeper trust and rapport.

That said, there are still many countries I haven't visited. I look forward to future travels, learning even more, and connecting with people from different backgrounds. After all, experiencing culture firsthand isn't just about seeing new places—it's about understanding new perspectives.

What cultural insight have you learned that changed how you see the world?

"It is the greatest of all mistakes
to do nothing because
you can only do little—
do what you can."

—*Sydney Smith*

19

The Power of Small Actions

Early in my career, one of my mentors shared the parable of the boy and the starfish during a particularly challenging company-wide initiative deployment. You've probably heard the story, but just in case, here it is in full:

A man was walking along a beach one morning after a storm. The shoreline was littered with thousands of starfish that had been washed ashore. Without the water, they would die. As he walked, he noticed a boy picking up starfish one by one and throwing them back into the ocean. Curious, the man approached the boy and said, "There are so many starfish here. You can't possibly save them all. What difference can you make?" The boy picked up another starfish, threw it into the water, and replied, "It made a difference to that one."

Small Efforts, Big Impact

This story illustrates the power of individual action and the importance of making a difference, even when the larger problem feels overwhelming. It reminds us that while we may not be able to solve every problem or help everyone, our actions can still have a meaningful impact—whether it's for one person, one moment, or one cause.

In this story, the starfish represents a challenge or problem. But what if we think of the starfish as a day instead? Life often throws overwhelming obstacles our way, leaving us stressed and uncertain about how to move forward. It's easy to feel paralyzed by what needs to be done. But just like the boy in the story, we can take it one day at a time.

The ocean in the story symbolizes hope and progress, reminding us that small efforts can create ripples of positivity around us. We don't need to fix everything at once—we just need to keep moving forward. No one has a perfect day, and we may not solve every issue. However, each day is part of a journey; the key is to approach it positively and determinedly.

What is your starfish—how will you make a difference today?

"It is not enough to be busy.
So are the ants. The question is:
What are we busy about?"

—*Henry David Thoreau*

20

The Danger of Solving the Wrong Problem

I've done quite a bit of statistical analysis during school and in my early career. One thing that always stands out is that hypothesis testing is important in validating theories. But here's the thing—it's not perfect. Since we work with limited data, errors can happen, and they're categorized as Type 1 and Type 2 errors.

- Type 1 Error (False Positive): This happens when you believe something is true when it's not. For example, it's like saying someone is guilty when they're actually innocent.
- Type 2 Error (False Negative): This is the opposite—you miss something that is actually true. For instance, concluding someone is innocent when they're guilty.

Pretty straightforward, right? But here's where it gets interesting—another type of error that doesn't get talked about as much: Type 3 Error.

What's a Type 3 Error?

A Type 3 error happens when you solve the wrong problem or answer the wrong question. You might get valid results, but they are irrelevant because the problem wasn't framed correctly.

Here's a simple example. Imagine spending hours building a bridge to cross a river, only to realize it is shallow, and you could have just walked through it. The bridge works perfectly—it's just that you didn't need it in the first place. This is a Type 3 error in action: a well-executed solution that was unnecessary from the start.

How Do We Avoid It?

Type 3 errors aren't just theoretical—they happen constantly in business, personal life, and politics. When they do, they lead to wasted resources, unnecessary conflicts, and disappointing outcomes. Avoiding them requires a mindset shift: instead of rushing to solve a problem, take a step back to ensure you're addressing the right one.

Here are a few ways to prevent Type 3 errors:

- Communicate clearly with everyone involved to ensure alignment on the real goal.
- Take time to scope the problem and dig into what's truly happening.

- Validate your question or objective before jumping into solutions.

Whether you're analyzing data, tackling a project, or making a big decision, it's always worth pausing to ask: "Are we solving the right problem?"

"Stars can't shine without darkness."

—*Unknown*

21

Finding Clarity in the Darkness

Looking back, I remember a particularly challenging period when I often found myself gazing at the night or early morning skies, watching the stars. Those were uncertain times for me, filled with self-doubt, difficult decisions, and a constant search for direction. Yet, there was something undeniably comforting about the quiet brilliance of the stars. They were distant, yet constant, shining through the vast darkness above.

At the time, I lived in a relatively sparsely populated residential area, unlike big cities, so stargazing wasn't too difficult. Still, if I wanted to see the stars more clearly, I would drive beyond the residential lights, away from the artificial glow that dulled their shine. The light pollution acted like noise, disrupting the clarity and beauty of the stars. It wasn't until I reached a truly dark place that I could fully appreciate the night sky.

The Power of Removing Distractions

That experience taught me an important lesson about life. Just as the stars are best seen when the noise of manmade lights is removed, our goals, dreams, and the beauty of life become clearest when we eliminate the distractions that cloud our focus. The modern world is filled with distractions—constant notifications, endless demands, and the expectations of others pulling us in different directions. When we let this artificial "light" take over, it becomes harder to see what truly matters.

Clarity doesn't always come in the busiest or brightest moments. Sometimes, it emerges in solitude, in quiet reflection, in stepping away from the noise and giving ourselves the space to think deeply about what we truly want. In the same way the stars shine their brightest against the darkest skies, our purpose and direction often become clearest during life's toughest moments—if we take the time to look for them.

Take a moment tonight to look at the stars. Step away from the noise, embrace the quiet, and reflect on your North Star.

What distractions cloud your clarity, and how can you remove them to see what truly matters?

"A man who carries a cat by the tail learns something he can learn in no other way."

—*Mark Twain*

22

Lessons Only Experience Can Teach

This quote is humorous yet profoundly true— some lessons in life can only be learned through direct, often painful experience. Can you imagine carrying a cat by the tail? It's an obvious mistake, but if you do it, you'll quickly understand why it's a bad idea—far better than any warning could teach you.

Another quote I like is: "Experience is the hardest kind of teacher. It gives you the test first and the lesson afterward." Though often attributed to Oscar Wilde, its exact origin remains unclear. This saying resonates because it captures the reality that life often teaches us through trial and error. We don't always get to prepare—we're thrown into situations, and only afterward do we fully grasp their significance.

The Power of Learning Through Experience

Experience is often the best teacher, especially when it comes to learning from mistakes. Some of my biggest lessons have come through direct experience in both sports and my career. In soccer and racquetball, every mistake was an opportunity to improve, sharpening my skills for the next match. Professionally, my early career as a Quality and Reliability Engineer was all about working in black-and-white decision-making. But when I transitioned into leadership, I quickly realized that success was no longer just about logic and data—it was about working effectively with people. No textbook could have fully prepared me for that. Leadership, I learned, is something you can only truly master through doing.

The toughest lessons, however, have come from dealing with people. Some individuals turned out exactly as I expected, while others were completely different from who I thought they were. Relationships and friendships that once seemed solid sometimes faded when circumstances changed—whether it was due to career moves, status shifts, or life transitions.

Embracing Mistakes and Moving Forward

Ultimately, our mistakes and failures shape us, making us stronger and wiser. They build resilience and often lead to even greater success down the road. The key is to embrace them, and learn from others' mistakes to avoid unnecessary hardships.

So, what's your recent story of grabbing the cat's tail?

"The eagle does not fear the storm.
It simply spreads its wings
and rises above it."

—*Unknown*

23

Rising Above Adversity

Jim Thorpe was an American athlete, Olympic gold medalist, and a member of the Sac and Fox Nation. He was the first Native American to win a gold medal for the United States in the Olympics and is widely regarded as one of the most versatile athletes in modern sports history. Thorpe won two gold medals at the 1912 Summer Olympics in the pentathlon and decathlon and later excelled in professional football, baseball, and basketball. His natural athleticism and determination set him apart. In 1950, the Associated Press named him the greatest athlete of the first half of the 20th century, placing him decisively ahead of Babe Ruth.

The Story of the Mismatched Shoes

One of the most iconic images of Jim Thorpe is from the 1912 Olympics, showing him wearing two different socks and mismatched shoes. The story behind this image is a testament to his resilience. Just before his competition in Stockholm, someone stole his socks and shoes. With little time to spare, he found two mismatched shoes in a trash bin and adjusted by wearing an extra sock on one foot to make the larger shoe fit. Despite this setback, Thorpe went on to win two gold medals.

This moment captures the essence of perseverance. In an era where athletes increasingly depend on advanced technology and specialized equipment, Thorpe's achievements remind us that true greatness does not come from what we wear or use but from the strength and resolve within us. His determination to compete—regardless of the circumstances—demonstrates that success is about resourcefulness, grit, and a refusal to let obstacles stand in the way.

Lessons from Thorpe's Legacy

Life is filled with unexpected challenges that test our resolve. Yet, like Thorpe, we all have the ability to rise above difficulties with effort, persistence, and the right mindset. He didn't allow circumstances beyond his control to derail his focus—he adapted, found a solution, and excelled despite the setback.

Thorpe's story is a powerful reminder that obstacles are not the end of the road but an opportunity to demonstrate resilience. We don't always get to choose our circumstances, but we do get to choose how we respond to them. Like an eagle soaring above the storm, we can rise above challenges, adjusting and pushing toward our goals.

What obstacles are you facing now, and how can you adjust to rise above them?

"Great leaders don't just inspire; they invest in the development of those they lead."

—*Unknown*

24

The Right Environment for Growth

While a koi fish's genetic makeup ultimately determines its maximum size, its environment plays a crucial role in its growth. A koi raised in a small pond may remain stunted due to environmental stressors—limited space, competition for food, and poor water quality. Though it has the potential to grow much larger, the constraints of its surroundings hold it back. In contrast, koi raised in larger, more accommodating environments have the opportunity to reach their full size.

Leadership and Growth Go Hand in Hand

This concept applies directly to people's development. Everyone has a unique potential, but the environment they are placed in—whether at work, in leadership, or personal growth—determines how far they can go. Like a koi fish in a small pond, employees confined by restrictive leadership, limited opportunities, or lack of support may struggle to grow. A leader must remove barriers and provide the space, resources, and challenges that encourage development.

Nurturing growth varies from person to person. It might involve:

- Providing learning opportunities
- Assigning challenging projects
- Offering mentorship and guidance
- Encouraging transitions into new roles
- Allowing room for failures that lead to growth

The key is tailoring development strategies to the stage and needs of the individual. Just as koi fish flourish in the right pond, people thrive in environments where they feel supported, challenged, and empowered.

Creating that kind of environment is what separates good leaders from great ones. Leadership isn't just about inspiring—investing in people, fostering their development, and giving them the space to grow into their full potential. That's the essence of true leadership.

How are you creating an environment that encourages growth for the people you lead?

"Be nice to people on the way up
because you'll meet them
on the way down."

—*Wilson Mizner*

25

The Full Circle of Life

With everything going on in the world, this quote has been on my mind. Attributed to American playwright and entrepreneur Wilson Mizner, it serves as a timeless reminder to be kind and respectful to everyone, regardless of their social status or position. Life is unpredictable, and no matter how successful someone becomes, they may one day need help from the people they once overlooked.

Kindness and Leadership Go Hand in Hand

This advice is often shared with those just starting their careers or building their businesses. It's especially relevant in competitive environments like corporate leadership and politics, where focusing only on personal gain can be tempting. But as Maya Angelou wisely said, "People will forget what you said, people will forget what you did, but people will never forget how you made them feel."

Some might argue that success in business requires pragmatism over kindness, but these two things are not mutually exclusive. Treating people with dignity, fairness, and respect doesn't mean sacrificing ambition or results—it means leading with integrity. When leaders create a culture of professionalism and kindness, they build stronger teams, earn loyalty, and foster lasting relationships beyond immediate business needs.

Success Is Temporary; Character Is Permanent

Life is full of ups and downs. Success is never guaranteed, and setbacks are inevitable. How we treat people during both the highs and the lows defines our true character. When we show kindness and humility in moments of triumph, we build goodwill. When we remain gracious and respectful in difficult times, we create a support system to lift us back up.

Ultimately, this is a call to embrace kindness and respect as guiding principles—personal or professional. The world is smaller than we think, and how we treat people today will shape our opportunities and relationships tomorrow.

Who in your life or career do you owe gratitude to for helping you along the way?

> "Courage is not the absence of fear, but the capacity to act despite our fears."

—*John McCain*

26

Leading Through the Storm

S ir Ernest Shackleton was a renowned Anglo-Irish explorer best known for his leadership during the Antarctic expeditions of the early 20th century, particularly the Imperial Trans-Antarctic Expedition (1914-1917). Despite his ship, the *Endurance*, becoming trapped and ultimately destroyed by ice, Shackleton's extraordinary leadership ensured the survival of his entire crew through one of history's most harrowing adventures.

Shackleton set out to be the first to cross Antarctica on foot, but by January 1915, *Endurance* became trapped in thick Antarctic pack ice, 100 miles from its intended landing point. For months, the ship drifted until immense pressure crushed it, forcing Shackleton and his 27 crew members to abandon the vessel before it sank.

Stranded on ice floes, the crew endured freezing conditions for months, surviving on salvaged supplies and three small lifeboats. When their ice floe broke apart in April 1916, they launched the lifeboats, braving treacherous seas to reach the barren shores of Elephant Island. Knowing survival on the island was unsustainable, Shackleton and five others undertook an extraordinary 800-mile journey across the Southern Ocean in a small lifeboat, reaching South Georgia Island. After trekking across its mountainous terrain, Shackleton secured a rescue vessel.

After multiple failed rescue attempts, Shackleton finally returned to Elephant Island on August 30, 1916, successfully saving all 22 stranded men. Despite impossible odds, not a single life was lost.

Reflecting on the expedition, Shackleton later said:

"In memories, we were rich. We had pierced the veneer of outside things. We had suffered, starved, and triumphed, groveled down yet grasped at glory, grown bigger in the bigness of the whole. We had seen God in His splendors and heard the text that Nature renders. We had reached the naked soul of men."

Though Shackleton never achieved his original goal, his expedition became a defining story of resilience, adaptability, and leadership under extreme circumstances. His ability to lead through uncertainty, unify his team, make decisive choices, and put his people first transformed a disaster into an extraordinary tale of survival.

Shackleton believed that "Optimism is true moral courage." He lived by this principle, leading his men with hope and determination despite overwhelming adversity. Today's leaders—whether in business, politics, or crisis situations—need that same mindset to navigate challenges and inspire others. Shackleton's story is more than a survival tale; it's a blueprint for leadership in adversity. His example challenges us to ask:

How could Shackleton's resilience, decisiveness, and commitment to his team inspire your own leadership?

"Alone, we can do so little;
together, we can do
so much."

—*Helen Keller*

27

The Strength of Many

G iant sequoias, also known as giant redwoods, are among the largest and oldest trees on Earth. Towering over 300 feet tall and weighing more than 2,000 tons, these trees are marvels of nature. Yet, despite their massive size, their roots are surprisingly shallow—only about 6 to 12 feet deep. So how do they remain standing for thousands of years?

Their secret isn't in their depth—it's in their connections. Sequoias spread their roots outward, intertwining with neighboring trees to form a vast, interdependent support system. This underground network provides stability and strength, allowing them to withstand storms, fires, and even earthquakes.

Lessons from the Giant Sequoia

Much like these trees, we are stronger together than we are alone. Their survival offers valuable leadership and life lessons:

1. Interconnected Support – Like Sequoia roots interlock for stability, strong teams,

organizations, and communities thrive on connection and trust. During challenging times, our relationships anchor us, keeping us steady when storms arise. No one succeeds alone.

2. Adaptability – Sequoias adjust to different soil conditions, finding ways to absorb nutrients despite their shallow roots. Likewise, resilient individuals and teams embrace change, continuously learning and adapting to new challenges.

3. A Strong Foundation – The massive trunks of these trees lower their center of gravity, improving their stability. In our own lives, a strong foundation—built on values, discipline, and trust—ensures that no matter how high we aim, we remain grounded and resilient.

Growing Together

The lesson of the giant sequoia is clear: our strength doesn't come from standing alone—it comes from growing together. When we build supportive relationships, stay adaptable, and establish strong foundations, we don't just survive—we thrive. Just as these towering trees have stood for millennia, we too can stand the test of time—if we stand together.

Who are the people in your life or work who keep you rooted, and how can you strengthen those connections?

"The influence of a mother in the lives of her children is beyond calculation."

—*James E. Faust*

28

The Profound Influence of Women

My mom was born in 1943 in Seoul, Korea. When the Korean War broke out, she was eight years old. Her father (my grandfather) ran a successful and wealthy business despite the war. My mom was smart and strong, excelling in high school, where she became her class's Vice President (apparently, the President role was reserved for a boy).

Before graduating from high school, a major fire destroyed her father's business. Since he had no insurance, the family lost everything. It was still not long after the war, and times were tough. Because society was male-dominated and favored sons, my mom had to give up her dream of attending college so that her younger brothers could pursue their education, given the family's financial struggles.

I liked my grandfather. He was intelligent and read books every day until he lost his eyesight. He passed away just before turning 100. In my mind, he was different from other men in society then, which made me very curious about why he chose not to send his eldest daughter to college. But I never asked him.

When I first heard this story as a child, it broke my heart. My mom was talented, yet she never had the chance to pursue her dreams because of societal and family expectations. However, she is incredibly smart and resilient. She overcame many challenges throughout her life and raised her children well, for the most part. She had a strong desire for education, likely because of what happened to her, and that influenced me profoundly, even without my realizing it. Her other qualities also shaped me and played a significant role in what I have experienced and where I am today.

My mom has been the most significant influence in my life, and this extends to other moms as well. In many cases, behind every successful person, a mother believed in them first. Mothers are strong—they protect their children, shape their values, and guide them toward success. Often, they juggle countless responsibilities to make everything happen, especially for their children. I don't want to generalize, but for the most part, this holds true.

My wife is another example. After many years of struggle, we finally had a baby—our daughter. She gave up her career as a professional pianist (I bear some responsibility for this due to our many job-related relocations) to care for our daughter full-time. It was often exhausting, managing everything day and night without much time for herself. Because of her dedication, our daughter thrives and has even taken up the violin, which she plays beautifully.

The sacrifices and dedication of mothers often go unnoticed, yet their influence shapes generations. Mothers leave an indelible mark on their children's lives, whether through the lessons they teach, the dreams they nurture, or the quiet strength they provide. I have seen this firsthand with my mom and my wife—two incredible women whose love and perseverance have shaped not just their families but the future. Success is rarely achieved alone; more often than not, a mother's unwavering belief, patience, and hard work are behind it. For that, I am deeply grateful.

Who is the woman who has influenced you the most, and in what ways?

"Hardships often prepare
ordinary people for an
extraordinary destiny."

—*C.S. Lewis*

29

The Power of the Boat

The Boys in the Boat (2023), directed by George Clooney, is a sports drama based on Daniel James Brown's book of the same name. It tells the inspiring true story of the University of Washington's rowing team and their improbable journey to Olympic gold at the 1936 Summer Games in Berlin. I watched this movie on a long flight to Asia. While enjoyable and uplifting, it felt old-fashioned and predictable, so I wouldn't call it a great film. However, its deeper lessons on teamwork, trust, and leadership left a lasting impression.

The Underdog Story

Set against the backdrop of the Great Depression, the story highlights the clash between socioeconomic classes. The main character, Joe Rantz (played by Callum Turner), is a working-class student who faces relentless teasing from wealthier peers for his worn-out clothing and modest background. Despite these challenges, he finds camaraderie with teammates who also come from humble beginnings.

Rowing was traditionally seen as a "rich man's sport," but Joe and his teammates shattered expectations through sheer grit, resilience, and hard work. Their journey wasn't just about rowing—it was about proving that determination can defy social barriers.

At one point, Joe nearly quits the team. In a pivotal conversation, Coach Al Ulbrickson (played by Joel Edgerton) delivers a powerful lesson on teamwork:

> **Coach Al Ulbrickson:** "Listen, I know it isn't easy to trust everyone on the boat as much as you trust yourself. But it's not about you. As good as you are, it's not about you, Joe, or me, or anybody else. It's about the boat."

> **Joe Rantz:** "Yes, sir. It's where I want to be."

This moment captures the essence of teamwork. Trust is not optional—it's essential. Individual talent means nothing if the team isn't aligned and working as one.

Lessons in Leadership and Resilience

Joe's working-class background shaped his toughness, focus, and perseverance—qualities that became strengths for the team. However, it wasn't just his resilience that made him a champion; it was his willingness to trust and be trusted. The story is a powerful reminder that:

- Talent alone isn't enough—teamwork is everything.
- Shared struggles build unbreakable bonds.
- True leadership isn't about individual glory but about elevating the entire team.

At its core, *The Boys in the Boat* is about the transformative power of trust and unity. When a group of individuals commit to something greater than themselves, they become unstoppable.

Do you fully trust the people on your left and right in your team?

"We can miss the real meaning of life if we get stuck climbing the wrong ladder."

—*Hope for the Flowers*

30

Climbing the Right Ladder

Hope for the Flowers is a beautifully written allegory by Trina Paulus, first published in 1972. I first read it at 14 in a Korean translation. It was simple, yet it left a profound impression on me. Years later, I revisited it in English as an adult, and while the story remained the same, its impact shifted significantly after I had spent time in the workforce.

Though often categorized as a children's book, *Hope for the Flowers* carries wisdom far beyond childhood. It speaks to ambition, purpose, and the search for fulfillment—themes that resonate with anyone at any stage of life.

A Tale of Two Caterpillars

The story follows two caterpillars, Stripe and Yellow, on their journeys of self-discovery.

- Stripe is restless, believing there must be more to life than simply eating leaves. He stumbles upon a pillar of caterpillars desperately climbing to reach "the top" and joins them, hoping to find meaning.

- Yellow also joins the climb but feels deeply uncomfortable stepping on others to get ahead. She and Stripe abandon the pillar and live together briefly, but Stripe's curiosity eventually pulls him back to the climb.

- After struggling to the top, Stripe finds nothing there—just more caterpillars still trying to climb. The success he chased turns out to be empty and unfulfilling.

- Meanwhile, Yellow follows her instincts, learning to build a cocoon and transform into a butterfly. She discovers the true way to the sky isn't through competition but through transformation.

- When Stripe returns, discouraged and lost, Yellow shows him her empty cocoon, inspiring him to undergo his own transformation. Soon, he becomes a butterfly, and they finally take flight together.

The Real Message Behind the Climb

The story's themes feel even more relevant in today's fast-paced, achievement-driven world.

Many of us start our careers like Stripe—chasing a vague idea of "success" without truly understanding what it means or where it leads. We climb ladders because society tells us to, only to find that the view from the top isn't what we imagined. The competition, the stepping on others, the sacrifices—sometimes, it all leads to an empty peak.

Meanwhile, Yellow represents a different kind of growth that comes from within. She trusts her instincts, embraces change, and finds her true purpose. She learns that real success isn't about climbing over others but about becoming who you are meant to be.

This story serves as a powerful reminder that success is not one-size-fits-all. The path that works for someone else may not be right for you. True fulfillment isn't about getting to the top but finding purpose, meaning, and transformation.

So, are you climbing the right ladder, or is it time to step back and find a different way to soar?

"There is a crack in everything;
that's how the light gets in."

—*Leonard Cohen*

31

The Beauty in Brokenness

Imagine holding a once-broken teacup, its cracks now traced with shimmering veins of gold. Instead of being discarded, it has been carefully repaired—not to hide its past, but to honor it. This is Kintsugi (金継ぎ), the Japanese art of golden repair, a practice that transforms broken pottery into something even more beautiful than before.

Kintsugi dates back to the 15th century when Shogun Ashikaga Yoshimasa sent his favorite tea bowl to China for repairs. It was returned crudely stapled together, leaving him disappointed. Seeking a more elegant solution, he turned to Japanese craftsmen, who developed a technique using lacquer mixed with powdered gold, silver, or platinum. Rather than trying to disguise the cracks, they highlighted them, creating a piece that was not just repaired but reborn.

The Philosophy of Kintsugi

At its core, Kintsugi embodies wabi-sabi—the Japanese philosophy that finds beauty in imperfection, change, and the passage of time.

- Wabi reflects simplicity and appreciation of the small moments in life.
- Sabi embraces aging, the character that time and experience bring.

Together, they remind us that perfection isn't the goal—growth is. The golden seams of Kintsugi don't just fix what was broken; they celebrate it. Each crack tells a story, a testament to resilience rather than a reminder of weakness.

A Lesson for Life

We all experience struggles, loss, and setbacks. The world often tells us to hide our scars, to smooth over the cracks, and to present an image of perfection. But Kintsugi teaches a different lesson: Our flaws don't diminish us. They define us.

The struggles we overcome, the pain we heal from, the lessons we learn—these are what make us unique and stronger than before. To heal is not to erase the past but to embrace it and become even more extraordinary.

The next time you feel discouraged by your imperfections, remember the golden seams of Kintsugi. Like a bowl repaired with gold, you are not less because of your struggles. You are more because you have overcome them.

What cracks in your own life could become a source of strength and beauty?

"Leadership has its costs.
You will often work harder
than anyone else, endure more
criticism, and give up personal
comforts for the greater good."

—*Craig Groeschel*

32

The Costs of Leadership

Kirby Smart, head coach of the University of Georgia, led his team to back-to-back national championships in 2021 and 2022. In one of his talks, he discussed the hidden aspects of leadership—the costs that great leaders must be willing to accept. He highlights three specific ones:

1. You must make hard decisions that could negatively affect the people you care about.
2. You will be disliked despite your best attempts to do the best for the most.
3. You will be misunderstood and won't always have the opportunity to defend yourself.

The Weight of Leadership

These insights hit me hard because they ring so true. Leadership isn't just about vision and inspiration—it comes with hard choices, criticism, and moments of isolation. At times, you will face decisions where there are no easy answers, only the best possible choice given the circumstances.

Smart emphasizes that in these moments, it's critical to lead with compassion and empathy. However, these costs prevent many talented individuals from stepping into leadership roles. Others may rise in leadership during good times but struggle when real challenges appear.

Leadership Isn't About Being Liked

One of the hardest lessons is that leadership isn't about pleasing everyone. It's not your job to make every person happy. Even when you are disliked, your responsibility is to do what is right—especially with the long-term outcome in mind. Compromising your standards or values just to win favor will ultimately weaken your leadership.

Every leader will face criticism—especially when tough decisions don't yield immediate or expected results. People will second-guess choices without fully understanding the factors involved. It's easy to say, "What if we had done this instead?" but much harder to offer real solutions at the moment. This is why surrounding yourself with an inner circle of truth-tellers is essential.

Leading Through Uncertainty

Leadership also means navigating transitions where clear communication isn't always possible. While transparency is important, there will be times when certain details can't be shared, leaving some individuals feeling uncertain or even resentful. This is another cost of leadership—being misunderstood without the ability to explain everything. I've personally experienced this reality in my career. Leadership can be a lonely place. But even in those difficult moments, there are always people who stand by you.

Are you willing to embrace the costs of leadership, even when the decisions are hard and the path is lonely?

"

"Sport has the power
to change the world. It has
the power to inspire. It can unite
people in a way that
little else does."

—*Nelson Mandela*

"

33

The Power of Unity

One of the most recognizable phrases in college sports is the iconic chant: "WE ARE ... PENN STATE." As a proud Penn State alumnus, I'm biased, but this chant is more than just words. It represents pride, tradition, and the unshakable bond that connects us as Penn Staters. Whenever I travel wearing Penn State gear—a hat, a sweatshirt, or anything with the school's logo—it's almost guaranteed that someone will call out, "WE ARE...," to which I enthusiastically respond, "PENN STATE!" It's a tradition I uphold every time I see another Penn Stater, no matter where I am.

A Tradition That Sticks

A particularly funny memory of this tradition happened shortly after I got married. My wife and I were touring a winery in Napa, California. At one point, I stepped away, leaving her alone wearing a Penn State t-shirt. Suddenly, a group of people spotted her and shouted, "WE ARE...!"

Since my wife isn't a Penn State graduate and is unfamiliar with the custom, she had no idea how to respond. She just stood there, bewildered, as the group waited. Needless to say, the moment fell flat. When I returned, she told me what happened, and I laughed hard before giving her a quick lesson on how to reply properly. Now, she's got it down and can confidently respond on her own!

How It All Started

According to Penn State historian Lou Prato, the chant "WE ARE… PENN STATE" was introduced by cheerleaders at Beaver Stadium in 1976. Inspired by the enthusiasm of opposing fans at away games, they wanted to create a call-and-response chant that would rally Penn State's crowd. They added a deliberate pause to encourage interaction, and by 1981, it had become a permanent and cherished part of Penn State culture. However, while the chant itself started in the '70s, the spirit behind it goes back much further.

One of the defining moments of Penn State's commitment to unity came in 1946 when the football team was scheduled to play against the then-segregated University of Miami. The team was told that if they wanted to compete, they would need to leave behind their two Black players, Wally Triplett and Dennie Hoggard. Instead of complying, the team made a bold choice: they refused to play.

The following year, Penn State went undefeated and received an invitation to the Cotton Bowl. Once again, they were told to leave Triplett and Hoggard behind. But the team remained united. Captain Steve Suhey reportedly declared, "We're Penn State," emphasizing that either the whole team played or none of them did.

The full team traveled to Dallas for the Cotton Bowl on January 1, 1948, where Triplett and Hoggard became the first African Americans to play in the Cotton Bowl. Triplett's game-tying touchdown helped secure a 13-13 draw against SMU, and he later made history as the first African American draftee to play in the NFL.

A Legacy That Still Matters

More than 75 years later, this story remains a powerful reminder of unity, inclusion, and standing together for what is right. While society has made significant progress since then, there is always more work to be done.

This story is bigger than Penn State—it's about what it means to stand firm in your values, to choose unity over division, and to create a culture where everyone belongs. I hope it resonates with people beyond the Penn State community, inspiring them to stay connected and stand together now more than ever.

What traditions, values, or moments of unity have shaped who you are today?

"If I had to go into a jungle, I'd want
to go with someone I could
trust with my life."

—*Unknown*

34

The People You Trust

I first came across a similar quote years ago, and it has stuck with me ever since. It's a powerful lens through which I evaluate whether someone is truly trustworthy—whether as a friend, a colleague, or a business partner.

This quote is often attributed to General William Tecumseh Sherman, though there's no verifiable record of him saying it. Others, including General James Mattis, have expressed similar sentiments. Regardless of its origin, the meaning is clear: when facing the unknown, when stepping into the "jungle"—you want to be alongside someone you trust completely. Someone you know will stand by you, protect you, and ensure survival in a life-or-death situation.

The Power of Trust in Leadership and Life

Trust is not just important in combat or survival scenarios—it is the foundation of any strong relationship, whether personal or professional. When the stakes are high, whether in business, leadership, or friendship, the people who prove to be reliable before, during, and after a crisis are the ones who matter most. Identifying these people in advance is essential. You don't want to wait until you're deep in the jungle to realize you're with the wrong person.

The best leaders understand that trust isn't just about surrounding themselves with competent people—it's about finding those who will stand by them through thick and thin. It's not about blind loyalty or unquestioning agreement. True trust is having people around you who will challenge you when necessary, who will speak up when they see danger ahead, and who will always prioritize doing what's right over what's easy.

Vulnerability: A Strength in Leadership

There's another critical element in choosing someone you'd trust in the jungle: vulnerability. Entrusting someone with your life means admitting that you can't do everything alone. This is just as true in leadership. Some believe that strong leadership means always having the answers, but in reality, great leaders are the ones who are willing to lean on others, admit when they need help, and create an environment where mutual trust thrives.

When a leader shows vulnerability, it doesn't weaken their authority—it strengthens it. It fosters respect, deepens connections, and creates a culture where people feel safe enough to be honest, take initiative, and challenge the status quo when needed.

Ultimately, trust, reliability, and vulnerability are not just abstract ideals—they are the foundation of meaningful relationships and effective leadership. Leaders who embrace these qualities not only navigate challenges more successfully but also build stronger, more resilient teams by inspiring those around them to grow and thrive. Whether in personal relationships or professional settings, the ability to trust and be trusted, to lead with integrity, and to show vulnerability are what ultimately define enduring success.

If you were heading into the jungle today, who would you want by your side, and why?

"You can pick your nose,
but you can't pick your boss."

—*Unknown*

35

The Leader You Get vs. The Leader You Become

I first heard this saying early in my career as part of some lighthearted career advice, and it stuck with me ever since. It's a humorous phrase, but it holds a deeper truth: we don't always get to choose who leads us.

From an employee's perspective, this reality can feel frustrating. We've all encountered leaders with different styles, personalities, and levels of competence. Some bosses inspire and empower, while others make every day a challenge. But while you **can't control** who your boss is, you **can** control how you navigate the relationship.

A saying that resonates with me is: The bad news is people don't change; the good news is people don't change.

While not entirely true, there's wisdom in it. People are who they are. Learning to understand your boss's strengths, weaknesses, and working style can help you find ways to align, communicate effectively, and get things done. Developing this adaptability is an invaluable career skill—it teaches you how to work with different leadership styles and make the most of any situation.

However, there are limits. If the environment becomes toxic or compromises your core values, it may be time to explore other options—whether seeking a new role within the company or stepping away entirely. The key is knowing when to adapt and when to move on.

When You ARE the Boss

Now, let's flip the perspective: what does this saying mean when **you** are the leader?

If your team members frequently express frustration about their leadership, it's a red flag. It suggests there may be gaps in your leadership approach and presents an opportunity for self-reflection and growth. A great leader doesn't just manage tasks—they inspire, guide, and support their team. While leadership styles vary, certain qualities remain **timeless and universal**:

- **A Clear Vision** – Great leaders define what success looks like and guide their team toward it.
- **Integrity** – Leading with honesty and consistency fosters trust and credibility.

- **Compassion** – Understanding the challenges and motivations of your team creates connection and loyalty.

Leadership that is built on trust and well-being is far more impactful than leadership at others' expense. The most effective leaders don't demand results—they empower people to achieve them.

At its core, leadership isn't just about achieving goals—it's about the relationships you build, the environment you create, and the impact you leave behind. You may not always get to pick your boss, but you can choose the kind of leader you become.

How will you lead in a way that inspires others and reflects your best self?

"Sometimes, the most ordinary things could be made extraordinary, simply by doing them with the right people."

—*Elizabeth Green*

36

The Power of the Right People

Even the simplest activities can become special and meaningful when shared with the right people. This applies not only to our personal lives but also to the workplace. In a professional setting, even routine tasks can become more impactful, enjoyable, and successful with the right team. A strong, supportive team fosters creativity, motivation, and a shared sense of purpose, turning everyday work into something truly extraordinary. This highlights the power of collaboration and the importance of working with people who complement and uplift each other.

However, we don't always recognize the right people or their talents. As a result, underutilized skills go to waste—a significant loss for any organization. A key responsibility of a leader is to identify talent and either maximize its potential or nurture its development.

Seeing the Potential in Others

In 1992, Steve Jobs spoke to students at the MIT Sloan School of Management. When asked, "What's the most important thing that you learned at Apple that you're doing at NeXT?" he responded after a long pause:

> "I now take a longer-term view on people. In other words, when I see something not being done right, my first reaction isn't to go fix it. It's to say we're building a team here and we're going to do great stuff for the next decade, not just the next year. And so, what do I need to do to help, so that the person that's screwing up learns vs. how do I fix the problem. And that's painful sometimes, and I still have that first instinct to go fix the problem, but that's taking a longer-term view on people, which is probably the biggest thing that's changed."

This underscores the importance of recognizing and developing talent to build a strong team for the long run. Jobs understood this and used it to build Apple into a great company—his lasting legacy behind the scenes.

As you know by now, I love cooking, and surprisingly, the *Kung Fu Panda* series is one of my favorites. A quote from *Kung Fu Panda 4* resonates deeply with me. Po tells Zhen: "Sometimes the greatest dishes come from the most unlikely ingredients."

This reminds us that remarkable outcomes often come from unexpected people and talents. Throughout my career, I've experienced this firsthand. And also, leaders took a chance on me, and I proved myself by delivering results. So let's focus on people. Let's give them opportunities, develop their potential, and let them shine.

What are the "unlikely ingredients" in your life that have surprised you?

"Critics are men who watch
a battle from a high place then
come down and shoot
the survivors."

—*Ernest Hemingway*

37

Step Into the Arena

It is not the critic who matters. It is not the one standing on the sidelines, casting judgment from a safe distance. True achievement belongs to those who step into the arena—those who dare to try, who stumble and rise again. The world is full of voices eager to tear down, but none matter more than the voice within—the one that knows your purpose, your effort, and your journey.

The loudest critics are often those who never dared to do what you are doing. They risk nothing, build nothing, and yet, they judge. But growth doesn't come from their opinions; it comes from action, from perseverance, from choosing to move forward even when doubt and difficulty stand in your way.

The Difference Between Spectators and Builders

Critics will always have something to say. They dissect decisions they never had to make, mock risks they were too afraid to take, and measure others by standards they never held themselves to. But history does not remember those who stood on the sidelines. It remembers the ones who showed up, who dared, who pushed forward despite the noise.

Theodore Roosevelt captured this truth perfectly:

"It is not the critic who counts... The credit belongs to the man who is actually in the arena, whose face is marred by dust and sweat and blood... who errs, who comes short again and again... but who does actually strive to do the deeds; who knows great enthusiasms, the great devotions; who spends himself in a worthy cause... so that his place shall never be with those cold and timid souls who neither know victory nor defeat."

So let the judgment of others fade. Let their doubt, their cynicism, and their criticism fall away. Focus instead on the work ahead, the goals you set, and the passion that drives you. It is far better to fail while daring greatly than to live in fear of failure, never having tried at all.

Will you let the fear of criticism hold you back, or will you step into the arena?

"Good friends are like stars. You don't always see them, but you know they're always there."

—*Unknown*

38

The Bonds That Time Can't Break

I recently had dinner with Frank Li, a good friend and former colleague from my days at Caterpillar. It had been a long time since we last saw each other, but the moment we sat down, it felt like no time had passed at all. He was passing through on a business trip, and we made sure to take the opportunity to reconnect.

In Chinese, there's a special term for a friend like him: 老朋友 (lǎo péngyǒu), meaning "old friend." It doesn't refer to age, but rather to the deep bond of a friendship that withstands time and distance. As we talked, I was reminded of a beautiful line from the Tang Dynasty poet Wang Bo (王勃) in his famous work, *Preface to the Tengwang Pavilion* (滕王阁序):

海内存知己，天涯若比邻.

Roughly translated, it means: "If you have a friend across the seas, even distant lands feel as close as neighbors."

True friendship isn't about proximity—it's about connection. No matter how much time passes or how far apart we are, some friendships remain strong, as if they were never interrupted.

Laughter, Memories, and Cracked Eggs

During dinner, another quote came to mind, from Bernard Meltzer, one that made me smile: "A true friend is someone who thinks that you are a good egg even though he knows that you are slightly cracked."

I'll admit, I may be more than *slightly* cracked, but that's what makes life interesting! We spent hours catching up—talking about business, our families, old colleagues, world events, and the future. Every dish tasted better because of the company, and time slipped away unnoticed. Eventually, we had to say goodbye. I wished him a safe journey back to Asia and left with a heart full of gratitude.

Moments like these remind me how **valuable true friendships are.** Life moves fast, and it's easy to lose touch. But the best friendships don't fade—they wait for us to pick up right where we left off.

When was the last time you reconnected with an old friend?

"An adult's greatest tragedy is forgetting that once, they too believed in magic."

—*The Little Prince*

39

Rediscovering Wonder

One of my favorite books is *The Little Prince* by Antoine de Saint-Exupéry. Though it appears to be a children's book, it carries profound lessons about human nature, relationships, and the way adults gradually lose their sense of wonder.

I first read it as a teenager, but every time I revisit it, I see it through a different lens. As a child, I was enchanted by the whimsical journey of the young prince. As an adult, I now recognize the deeper themes woven into the story—how we lose sight of what truly matters as we grow older.

The Flawed Grown-Ups We Become
During his journey, the Little Prince meets a series of adults, each representing a different flaw in human nature:

- **The King** rules over nothing but demands obedience, reflecting how people chase power and control, even when it is meaningless.

- **The Vain Man** craves admiration without real connection, reminding us of the emptiness of seeking validation from others.
- **The Drunkard** drinks to forget his shame, showing how people sometimes escape their problems rather than confront them.
- **The Businessman** obsessively counts stars, believing ownership gives him worth, symbolizing society's obsession with wealth at the cost of real joy.
- **The Lamplighter** follows outdated rules without question, representing blind obedience—even when change is needed.
- **The Geographer** gathers knowledge but never explores, embodying those who accumulate facts without ever truly experiencing life.

Each of these figures serves as a cautionary tale—reminders of what happens when we lose sight of imagination, joy, and deeper meaning.

Seeing the World Through a Child's Eyes

The Little Prince, in contrast, sees the world differently. He values love, friendship, and curiosity over power, possessions, or routine. He reminds us that what truly matters is often invisible to the eye—a lesson many adults forget.

As we grow up, we tend to trade wonder for practicality, replace curiosity with routine, and measure success by numbers instead of meaning. But *The Little Prince* challenges us to rediscover what we once knew as children—that magic still exists in the simplest things, if only we take the time to see it.

How can you bring a little more wonder back into your life?

"A daughter is one of the most
beautiful gifts this world
has to give."

—*Laurel Atherton*

40

The Greatest Gift

Life is made up of moments—some fleeting, others monumental—but few are as profoundly transformative as the birth of a child. The day my daughter was born, time seemed to stand still. I was enveloped in pure, unfiltered joy, as if the universe itself had paused to honor the arrival of this tiny, perfect life.

My wife and I married later in life, and for years, we struggled to have a baby. The journey was emotionally exhausting, especially for my wife. Then, after we repatriated to the U.S. following an overseas assignment, something miraculous happened—she became pregnant almost immediately. It felt like a blessing beyond words, a long-awaited answer to our prayers.

Because of our past struggles, we were cautious throughout the pregnancy. Every small concern loomed large. Each doctor's visit carried both anticipation and anxiety. But with every kick, every heartbeat on the monitor, we were reminded of the life growing within her—our greatest gift.

A Night That Changed Everything

It was an ordinary Sunday, three weeks before her due date. We spent the day cooking, chatting with neighbors, and enjoying a slow, peaceful afternoon. Then, that night, everything changed. Labor started unexpectedly. Unsure if it was real or a false alarm, we packed our bags and headed to the hospital—just in case.

Hours passed in a blur of pain and perseverance. My heart ached for my wife as she endured each contraction with unwavering strength. She was heroic, pushing through exhaustion with a determination that left me in awe. And then, in the quiet stillness of early Monday morning, she arrived.

Her first cries filled the room—a raw, beautiful declaration of life. When I saw her—so small, so perfect—I was overwhelmed by emotions I had never felt before. My wife held her first, and for a moment, the world disappeared. Every fear, every hardship, every long year of waiting faded, leaving only the breathtaking beauty of our daughter's first moments in the world.

A Love Beyond Words

When I finally held her in my arms, something inside me shifted. I felt an unshakable sense of love, responsibility, and gratitude. In that instant, I knew my life had changed forever. As my wife rested, I carried our daughter for her tests, holding her close, cherishing every second. It was pure joy, the kind that fills every corner of your soul.

Her birth was more than just the arrival of a new life—it was the beginning of a new chapter. In her, I saw **endless possibilities**—the dreams she would chase, the adventures she would embark on, the person she would become. That day, I understood the true meaning of joy and love in a way I never had before.

A Decade of Gratitude

She's ten years old now. Every time I hug her, I am transported back to that moment—the miracle of her birth, the overwhelming love that filled the room. The memory is etched into my heart, a guiding light on this incredible journey of parenthood.

Every day, I pray that she grows into a kind, strong, and compassionate person. That she pursues her dreams and leaves her mark on the world. No matter what challenges life brings, I know they will always be outweighed by the joy of that singular, blessed moment—the day I met my daughter for the first time.

What moment in your life has filled you with a love so profound that it changed you forever?

"A leader's power lies in having options. The moment you have only one choice, you are at the mercy of circumstances."

—*John C. Maxwell*

41

The Power of Options

Have you ever heard the phrase **"Hobson's choice"**? It refers to a situation where you have only one option—take it or leave it. The term comes from Thomas Hobson, a 16th-century stable owner who managed the workload of his horses by offering customers a single choice: take the horse nearest the door or take none at all. It created the illusion of choice when in reality, there was no real alternative.

A long time ago, I read about a tragic plane crash. The article mentioned that the pilot had faced a **Hobson's choice**—only one course of action, no real alternatives. That phrase stuck with me. While this was an extreme case, it made me think about how, in life, being forced into a single option rarely leads to a good outcome.

The same principle applies across personal life, business, and leadership. Jeff Bezos once said, "In business, the worst position to be in is one where you have no choice. Always create alternatives."

While he spoke in a business context, this idea is universally relevant. The ability to create **alternatives** gives us flexibility, power, and control. When we proactively seek options, we avoid feeling trapped by a single, limiting path.

Life Is a Game of Probabilities

It may sound cliché, but life is a game of probability. While we can't guarantee outcomes, we can **increase the odds** of achieving what we want by creating more choices. When we have options, we improve our chances of success rather than letting circumstances dictate our path. The key is to think ahead, anticipate challenges, and cultivate alternatives before we need them.

That said, I know life isn't always that simple. There are times when circumstances limit our choices. But the more we work to create **options**, the better positioned we are to shape our future rather than being shaped by it.

What alternatives can you create today that will help you take control of your own path, no matter the circumstances?

"Success is not the key to happiness. Happiness is the key to success. If you love what you are doing, you will be successful."

—*Albert Schweitzer*

42

Passion Fuels Success

I've always loved documentaries—especially those that tell powerful human stories. Several years ago, I watched *Scotch: A Golden Dream* (2018), a documentary about the craftsmanship, culture, and legacy of Scotch whisky. One of the central figures was industry legend Jim McEwan, a man who spent decades shaping the world of whisky.

At one point in the film, McEwan shared a thought that stuck with me. He said:

"The only consistent thing in your body from the day you were born until the day you die"—(he patted his chest, referring to his heart)—"it just never stops. It's consistent. So why would you not follow that?" By then, he had been in the industry for over 50 years. His longevity wasn't just due to skill or experience—it was fueled by passion. His work wasn't just a career; it was a calling.

The Best Moments Aren't About the Product— They're About the Experience

Another part of the documentary stood out to me. When people were asked about the best dram of whisky they'd ever had, their answers weren't about the rarest or most expensive bottles. Instead, they spoke of the moments:

- A drink shared with a father.
- A glass enjoyed with close friends.
- A sip by a warm fire on a cold night.
- The smell of whisky brings back a cherished memory.

It wasn't about *what* they drank, but *who* they shared it with.

This idea goes beyond whisky—it's the essence of life. At work, we don't just remember projects and promotions. We remember the people who stood beside us through the highs and lows. The colleagues who pushed us forward, the mentors who guided us, the teammates who celebrated and struggled with us. Those are the moments that last.

Putting Your Heart Into What You Do

Watching this documentary reinforced a lesson I've seen play out time and time again: when you put your heart into something, it makes all the difference—both for you and for the people around you.

In business, it's a reminder that success isn't just about the product; it's about the experience. Brands aren't built solely on what they sell but on the emotions and stories they create. The same is true for leadership. The best leaders aren't just focused on results—they build meaningful connections and create lasting impact.

What is a memorable experience—whether in work or life—that has stayed with you, not because of what happened, but because of who you shared it with?

“

"To raise new questions, new possibilities, to regard old problems from a new angle requires creative imagination and marks real advance in science."

—*Albert Einstein*

"

43

Seeing What's Missing

During World War II, Allied commanders analyzed bullet hole patterns on returning fighter planes. Their instinct was logical: reinforce the areas that showed the most damage. But mathematician Abraham Wald saw the flaw in their thinking. They were only looking at the planes that made it back.

The planes that didn't return were the ones hit in the most vulnerable spots. The key insight? The areas without bullet holes on surviving planes revealed the weak points, because when a plane was hit there, it didn't make it home. This realization changed aircraft reinforcement strategies and later influenced the design of the Skyraider during the Korean War. It's a powerful lesson in decision-making: sometimes, what's missing from the data tells us more than what we can see.

Challenging the Status Quo

This principle applies far beyond aviation. In business, leadership, and everyday life, we often fall into the trap of focusing only on what's visible, without questioning what's missing.

How many times have you heard, **"We've always done it this way"**? It's one of the most dangerous phrases in any organization. I've seen it firsthand in quality improvement projects—when I asked why things were done a certain way, no one could remember. The original reasoning may have made sense at the time, but as circumstances changed, the approach became outdated. Yet, because no one questioned it, inefficiencies persisted.

The Power of a Fresh Perspective

Einstein put it best: "You cannot solve a problem with the same mind that created it."

Real solutions require more than just doing things differently—they require thinking differently. Innovation happens when we challenge assumptions, approach problems from new angles, and recognize that the biggest insights often come from what's missing, not just what's in front of us.

What might you be overlooking today that was always there?

"Strong leaders have a fixed destination but are open to changing the route."

—*Simon Sinek*

44

Stubborn Vision, Flexible Path

We all set personal and professional goals but rarely do things go exactly as planned. In my experience, not once have I reached an important goal without encountering unexpected obstacles. There is always an unforeseen challenge, a necessary adjustment, or a lesson learned along the way.

From a leadership perspective, success isn't about rigidly following a single path. Instead, the best leaders balance **conviction with adaptability**—they remain steadfast in their purpose while staying flexible in their execution. This ability to adjust without losing sight of the destination is what allows them to navigate uncertainty, empower their teams, and drive continuous progress.

The Balance of Stubbornness and Flexibility

A few years ago, I came across an interview with Jeff Bezos, where he spoke about the critical balance between persistence and adaptability. He put it this way: "You need a combination of stubborn relentlessness and flexibility. And you have to know when to be which. Be stubborn about your vision; otherwise, it will be too easy to give up. But be flexible on the details, because as you go along pursuing your vision, you'll find that some of your preconceptions were wrong, and you're going to need to be able to change those things."

Bezos was speaking about entrepreneurship and product development, but his wisdom applies to leadership, business, and life. Goals provide direction, but the path to achieving them is rarely straight.

Adaptability in Leadership

The best leaders don't just set a vision; they constantly refine their strategies. In the business world, frameworks like the Plan-Do-Check-Act (PDCA) cycle help organizations assess progress, identify necessary adjustments, and pivot when needed. Leaders who cling too tightly to a fixed plan risk missing opportunities for improvement—or worse, leading their teams in the wrong direction.

My own career is a testament to this principle. When I started as a Quality and Reliability Engineer, I envisioned a long-term leadership role in that field. But as I grew, new opportunities reshaped my path. I had the privilege of working alongside inspiring leaders who expanded my perspective, leading me to opportunities I had never anticipated.

Despite these shifts, my commitment to growth and leadership never wavered. Instead of seeing changes as detours, I embraced them as part of the journey. Many of the achievements I was part of along the way continue to serve as stepping stones for future success.

Strategic planning isn't about predicting every step—it's about preparing for change. Strong leaders think ahead, build contingencies, and stay agile, ensuring they can adapt without losing sight of their ultimate goal.

How do you balance staying true to your vision while adapting to change in your own journey?

"The cold water does not get warmer if you jump late."

—*François de La Rochefoucauld*

45

The Cost of Waiting

So true, isn't it? This saying carries several powerful lessons. First, it reminds us that delaying action doesn't make a difficult or uncomfortable task any easier. Waiting for perfect circumstances is an illusion—challenges will always exist. Whether it's a tough decision, an intimidating project, or a personal goal, hesitation only prolongs discomfort. The sooner we take action, the sooner we adapt and move forward.

A second lesson is about time—one of our most precious and irreplaceable resources. Once a moment passes, it's gone forever. We often wish for more time, yet paradoxically, we waste it on indecision or fear. As Edward Young wisely put it, "Procrastination is the thief of time." Indeed, putting things off doesn't just delay progress; it robs us of opportunities and personal growth. Time is always moving, and it won't wait for us to be ready.

A third important aspect is **opportunity cost**. Every moment spent delaying action is a moment that could have been used productively elsewhere. Worse still, some opportunities are fleeting—by the time we finally decide to act, they may no longer be available. The job you hesitated to apply for, the investment you waited too long to make, the business idea you kept refining instead of launching—these delays can mean missing out entirely.

It's not always black and white. There are times when careful planning is necessary, but more often than not, overthinking leads to inaction. Success favors those who move decisively. This wisdom reminds us that time should be used wisely—before it slips away.

So, what actions are you postponing today?

"When fishermen cannot go
to sea, they repair nets."

—*Unknown Proverb*

46

Preparing for the Next Opportunity

The origins of this proverb may be unclear, but its wisdom is undeniable. When the sea is too rough, fishermen don't sit idly by. They mend their nets, sharpen their tools, and prepare for the next opportunity. They use downtime wisely, ensuring they're ready to seize the moment when the waters calm.

A similar principle is found in the Chinese saying, "Repair the roof while the weather is fair." The message is the same: Use quiet periods not as a time to wait, but as a time to prepare.

Applying This Wisdom to Life and Business

In life, setbacks—whether a job loss, an illness, or personal struggles—can feel like forced pauses. But these moments are also opportunities to reflect, learn, and strengthen ourselves. We can use them to develop new skills, nurture relationships, and invest in our physical and mental well-being. When I was building my consulting business, I embraced this mindset. I focused on personal growth, spent quality time with family and friends, and prioritized my health. That season of preparation paid off.

In business, slow periods can be frustrating, but they don't have to be wasted. Instead of focusing solely on cost-cutting, smart companies use downtime to:

- **Refine internal processes** – Streamline operations, eliminate inefficiencies, and improve workflows.
- **Train employees** – Develop skills, enhance team capabilities, and build a stronger workforce.
- **Innovate** – Explore new products, services, and markets.
- **Strengthen relationships** – Deepen connections with clients, partners, and employees.

When I was a plant manager, we used slow periods to tackle continuous improvement projects. This proactive approach not only increased efficiency but also positioned us for long-term success. Businesses that invest in development during downturns emerge stronger when the market rebounds.

Though downtime can be challenging, it's also a powerful opportunity. The key is to shift our perspective—not to see it as a pause, but as preparation for the next wave of opportunity.

How have you used periods of downtime to prepare for future success?

"And once the storm is over, you won't remember how you made it through, how you managed to survive. You won't even be sure whether the storm is really over. But one thing is certain. When you come out of the storm, you won't be the same person who walked in. That's what this storm's all about."

—*Haruki Murakami*

47

The Strength of the Storm

This quote resonates deeply with me because, like everyone else, I've faced my own storms— some small, some life-changing. Each one has tested me, shaped me, and made me stronger. Without those challenges, I wouldn't be the person I am today. Through them, I've learned persistence, resilience, and the wisdom of knowing when to take action and when to simply endure.

Looking back, two things stand out:

1. You Don't Have to Face the Storm Alone

I never weathered my storms on my own. Whether it was family, friends, colleagues, or mentors, I was surrounded by people who lifted me up when I needed it most. Throughout my career, I was thrown into unfamiliar roles, often in new cities or foreign countries. While I was grateful for the trust placed in me, my real confidence came from knowing I wasn't alone.

When you're facing a storm, don't assume you have to go it alone. Look around—your support system may be closer than you think.

2. Celebrate the Calm After the Storm

Every storm passes. And when it does, there is always something to celebrate—whether a big victory or a quiet moment of relief. Too often, we move on too quickly, forgetting to acknowledge how far we've come.

But celebration doesn't have to be extravagant. It can be a quiet dinner with family, a drink with colleagues, or a simple moment of gratitude. As Joél Leon puts it: "Please, don't forget to celebrate yourself—celebrate your wins, celebrate your growth, celebrate your recovery, celebrate your being. Celebrate yourself every day, even when you don't think you deserve to."

Yes, celebrate yourself. But also celebrate with those who stood beside you. They were part of the journey, too. Then, when the celebration ends, we move forward—stronger, wiser, and ready for whatever comes next.

So, what was your latest storm, and how did you celebrate the rainbow?

"

"The function of leadership is to produce more leaders, not more followers."

—*Ralph Nader*

"

48

The Human Side of Leadership

We tend to think of leadership as strategy, vision, or charisma. But what if the real magic of outstanding leadership is far more human and personal?

When I first came across the book *Trillion Dollar Coach: The Leadership Playbook of Silicon Valley's Bill Campbell* by Eric Schmidt, Jonathan Rosenberg, and Alan Eagle, I assumed it was about financial coaching—I was utterly wrong. The book explores the leadership principles and coaching philosophy of Bill Campbell, a former football coach turned executive coach, who mentored some of Silicon Valley's most successful leaders, including Steve Jobs, Larry Page, and Jeff Bezos.

Throughout the book, Bill Campbell shares his philosophy, which is all about People First, Teamwork, Candor, and Tough Love. His coaching style and approach are direct, yet he also focuses on listening, guiding, and challenging leaders. In the end, execution and decision-making matter. Here's what we can all learn from Campbell's "people first" philosophy.

It Starts with Trust

If you want to lead well, start by building trust. Not the kind earned after years of shared experiences, but the kind that creates safety from day one. That's what legendary executive coach Bill Campbell believed—and it's something every leader needs to understand.

Trust doesn't mean always agreeing. When trust is strong, disagreement becomes easier. People speak up. Ideas are shared. And real collaboration begins. If your team isn't really talking, it's worth asking if they feel safe enough to disagree.

As a leader, focusing on performance metrics, decisions, and outcomes is easy. But without trust, none of that matters. People follow leaders they believe in— and they believe in you when they know you care.

Coachability, Teamwork, and Real Impact

Campbell coached some of Silicon Valley's greatest minds—Jobs, Bezos, Page—not because he had the answers, but because he asked the right questions. He challenged them, guided them, and made them better. But there was one condition: they had to be coachable.

Are you?

Campbell believed that to get the most out of a coaching relationship, people must be coachable. He looked for honesty, humility, perseverance, hard work, and a constant openness to learning. A successful coaching relationship requires a high degree of vulnerability. Being coachable means staying willing to learn—even when you're already successful. It requires vulnerability. That's where the real growth happens.

Finally, remember that people often seek out "superheroes"—individuals with exceptional intelligence and skills who can seemingly do it all. However, Campbell argued that a team cannot function with only quarterbacks; it requires a diverse mix of talents woven together thoughtfully. "If you have the right person in the right job, you don't have to manage them. They will do great things," he wrote.

So, take a moment and reflect:

- Are you putting people first?
- Are you building trust—or just hoping for it?
- Are you coachable?
- Are you creating a team that can win together?

You don't need to be famous or in Silicon Valley to apply these lessons. You just need to care deeply about your people—and be brave enough to lead with trust, humility, and heart.

What's one thing you could do this week to lead more like that?

"

"We can't direct the wind,
but we can adjust the sails.
For maximum happiness, peace,
and contentment, may we choose
a positive attitude."

—*Thomas S. Monson*

"

49

Adjusting Your Sails

This quote has been attributed to many—Thomas S. Monson, Jimmy Dean, Dolly Parton— but no matter who said it first, the message remains powerful: We can't always control what happens to us, but we can control how we respond. Our attitude, our mindset, and our ability to adapt determine how far we go.

But before we can adjust our sails, we must first know where we're headed. As Seneca wisely said: "If one does not know to which port one is sailing, no wind is favorable."

That's the key—clarity. Whether in life, leadership, or business, we need a clear destination. I often call this our *North Star* or *Blue Dot.* Are we investing our time in the right things? Are we even on the right path? If the answer is yes, then resilience and adaptation become our tools for success. If the answer is no, it may be time to change direction—or step back and find the right course entirely.

Once we have our direction set, the next step is to embrace adaptability. As Randy Pausch put it: "We cannot change the cards we are dealt, just how we play the hand."

Every day presents challenges—some small, some major. Some days we win, some days we don't. But every tomorrow is another chance to adjust, improve, and move forward. In business, just like in life, clarity and self-awareness are everything. We need to assess where we are, recognize the gap between our current reality and our ultimate goal, and then take decisive action to bridge that gap.

So, as each day ends, take a moment to reflect:

- Was today a small win? A big one?
- Did I face setbacks? Major challenges?
- What adjustments do I need to make for tomorrow?

Because no matter how the wind blows, you have the power to adjust your sails.

The real question is: How will you adjust them tomorrow?

"

"Without change, there is no innovation, creativity, or incentive for improvement. Those who initiate change will have a better opportunity to manage the change that is inevitable."

—*William Pollard*

"

50

The Discipline of Continuous Improvement

For years, I maintained a disciplined workout routine that kept me in great shape. But as my career demands grew, frequent business trips and mounting stress took their toll. My workouts became inconsistent, my eating habits suffered, and before I knew it, my health was no longer a priority.

In 2024, I made a conscious decision to change that. I recommitted to disciplined exercise and better nutrition, realizing that if I didn't take control, my health would continue to decline. Looking back, I see a clear parallel between personal health and corporate health—both require consistent effort, accountability, and a commitment to improvement.

Like individuals, companies can fall into patterns of complacency, neglecting the long-term for the sake of short-term comfort. Without a proactive culture of continuous improvement, they risk losing their edge. This is where *Lean Culture* plays a critical role in sustaining success.

The Parallels Between Personal Health and Lean Leadership

1. **Recognizing the Need for Change**
    Just as I had to acknowledge my declining fitness, companies must recognize when they're losing their competitive edge. Sustainable success requires a mindset of continuous improvement. Lean organizations practice *Hoshin Kanri* (Policy Deployment) or other strategic alignment methods to ensure every level of the company is moving in the right direction, identifying challenges early, and preventing stagnation.

2. **Disciplined and Consistent Execution**
    A workout plan without consistency is useless—just like a business strategy that isn't followed through. Companies must adopt disciplined improvement processes like *Kaizen* (incremental improvements), *A3 problem-solving*, and *value stream mapping* to eliminate waste and enhance efficiency. Daily management practices such as *gemba walks* and *standardized work* keep execution on track.

3. **Monitoring Progress**
    In fitness, tracking progress keeps you accountable. In business, *key performance indicators (KPIs)* and *visual management tools* do the

same. But too many companies track *every-thing*—making it impossible to focus on what truly matters. Lean organizations prioritize *a critical few KPIs* that directly impact performance and customer value.

4. **Adapting to Challenges**
No fitness journey is without setbacks—plateaus, injuries, or unexpected life events require adjustments. Similarly, businesses must pivot when market conditions shift. Lean organizations use the *PDCA (Plan-Do-Check-Act) cycle* and root cause analysis (*5 Whys*) to diagnose problems and make necessary adjustments.

5. **Long-Term Commitment**
Sustainable health isn't about a quick fix—it's about making wellness a way of life. The same goes for business success. Lean isn't just a set of tools; it's a *culture* built on *continuous improvement (Kaizen)* and *long-term thinking (Hoshin Kanri)*. Companies that commit to this mindset create resilient, adaptable organizations that thrive over time.

My renewed focus on health didn't just strengthen me physically—it reinforced the importance of maintaining *organizational health*. Businesses that prioritize adaptability, improvement, and long-term strategy don't just survive—they lead.

"Are you proactively strengthening your personal and professional health, or are you waiting until decline forces you to change?"

"

Twenty years from now, you will be
more disappointed by the things
that you didn't do than by
the ones you did do.

So, throw off the bowlines.
Sail away from the safe harbor.
Catch the trade winds
in your sails.

Explore. Dream. Discover."

—*Mark Twain*

"

51

Sailing Toward Your Future

I didn't come across this quote until later in life, but when I did, it struck me deeply. At the time, I was considering a career change, and these words challenged me: Would I look back someday and regret not taking the leap? I wasn't fresh out of college, but that didn't matter—risk isn't just for the young. It's for anyone who refuses to settle for a life of "what-ifs." Looking back, I'm grateful I took the step.

Many of the world's most successful people didn't follow a traditional path. Some took risks early, leaving behind security to chase their dreams:

- Bill Gates (Microsoft) – Left Harvard in 1975 to co-found Microsoft.
- Steve Jobs (Apple) – Dropped out of Reed College and later transformed multiple industries.
- Mark Zuckerberg (Facebook) – Walked away from Harvard to build the world's largest social network.

- Michael Dell (Dell Technologies) – Started his company from a dorm room at 19.

But reinvention isn't just for the young. Many found their calling later in life, proving that it's never too late to change direction:

- Colonel Harland Sanders (KFC) – Built a global franchise at 65.
- Ray Kroc (McDonald's) – Transformed McDonald's into a powerhouse at 52.
- Arianna Huffington (The Huffington Post) – Launched her media empire at 55.
- Vera Wang (Fashion Designer) – Switched careers at 40.
- Momofuku Ando (Instant Ramen) – Invented instant noodles at 48, changing food history.
- Morris Chang (TSMC) – Founded the world's leading semiconductor company at 56.

Why do so many people hesitate to make bold moves later in life? Fear. Responsibilities. Uncertainty. It's easy to believe that big changes are only for the young, but that's simply not true. While you don't have to drop everything and start over, you do have to decide whether you're willing to step outside your comfort zone.

As John A. Shedd once wrote, "A ship in harbor is safe, but that is not what ships are built for."

You are that ship. You were built to move forward, to chase your North Star, to explore new waters. The path may not be easy, but the real question is:

Will you stay anchored in safety, or will you set sail toward your future?

"Write it on your heart
that every day is the best day
of the year.
He is rich who owns the day,
and no one owns the day
who allows it to be invaded
with fret and anxiety.

Finish every day and be
done with it.
You have done what you could.
Some blunders and absurdities,
no doubt crept in.
Forget them as soon as you can,
tomorrow is a new day;
begin it well and serenely,
with too high a spirit
to be cumbered with your
old nonsense.

This new day is too dear,
with its hopes and invitations,
to waste a moment on
the yesterdays."

—*Ralph Waldo Emerson*

52

The Power of Today

I'd like to end this book with one of my favorite passages—this beautiful and inspiring excerpt from Emerson. His words serve as a powerful reminder to embrace each day with a fresh perspective, free from the burdens of past mistakes and anxieties. Emerson speaks to mindfulness, resilience, and renewal—qualities that shape both life and leadership.

No one has a perfect day. Life brings both ups and downs, but we must choose to live in the present. The idea that "every day is the best day" challenges us to appreciate the moment rather than dwell on the past or worry about the future.

As Ernest Hemingway wrote in For Whom the Bell Tolls: "Today is only one day in all the days that will ever be. But what will happen in all the other days that ever come can depend on what you do today."

That's the key: what we do today matters. Let's fully own this day. Let's not allow stress, anxiety, or external pressures to take control of our time and energy. Mistakes and failures are inevitable, but they don't define us. What does? Our ability to move forward with clarity and determination.

As Jerry Falwell Sr. once said:

"You don't determine a person's greatness by their talent, wealth, or education. You determine a person's greatness by what it takes to discourage them."

Resilience in the face of adversity is what separates good from great. Yes, hopes and invitations—fresh new opportunities—await us every day. We should begin each day with a positive and purposeful attitude, refusing to be weighed down by past mistakes, regrets, or failures.

Are you living intentionally, free from negativity? What will you do with this new day?

www.ingramcontent.com/pod-product-compliance
Lightning Source LLC
Chambersburg PA
CBHW021924190326
41519CB00009B/897